THE PALGRAVE MURPHY SHIPPING LINE

1850-1926

For Rhona, who helped to rescue the past from itself.

The Shipping Murphys

THE PALGRAVE MURPHY SHIPPING LINE
1850-1926

Cornelius F. Smith

ALBANY PRESS

This book was typeset by
ASHFIELD PRESS PUBLISHING SERVICES
for

ALBANY PRESS
Blackrock • County Dublin
Ireland

ISBN: 0 954034 01 5

A catalogue record for this book is available from the British Library.

This book is typeset in 12 on 16 point Bembo

Printed in Ireland by
ßetaprint Limited, Dublin

Contents

DATE	PALGRAVE / MURPHY	DUBLIN EVENTS	GREAT BRITAIN AND ELSEWHERE
1882	Charles Palgrave res.London	Cavendish assassinated	
1884		Munster Bank in crisis	Franchise Act
1886	M. Murphy III to North Wall	Golf on Bull Island	Home Rule splits Liberals
1889	M. Murphy III – U.K. Cargo Service	Labour unrest until 1914	London Dock strike
1890		O'Shea divorce scandal	Gladstone opposes Parnell
1891		Redmond leads Irish Party	*Rerum Novarum*
1893	Charles Palgrave 1813-93	Marine Technical School, Dublin	Home Rule Bill rejected
1894	M. Murphy II 1816-94	Coal imports over 1 m. tons	Death Duties raised
1901		Royal Irish Automobile Club formed	Queen Victoria dies
1903		Land War ending	Wyndham Land Act
1907	Palgrave Murphy subscribes £250 to the Exhibition.	Exhibitions-Edward VII and Alexandra Hibernian Insurance Company formed	Company Consolidation legislation. Irish crown jewels scandal
1911	Sir James to 'Yapton'	Population 404,000	King Edward VII in Dublin
1912-13		Strikes *Titanic* sinks	Home Rule Rejected 1914
1914-18	Governments control ships. P.M. fleet disposed of.	Economic boom. Easter Rising 1916	Great War. *Leinster* torpedoed
1919	Heyn/Ulster S.S. Co. takes control of Palgrave Murphy	City of Dublin S.P.C. collapses into B & I	Treaty of Versailles
1922	Sir James 1843-1922	Treaty approved by I.F.S.	Amalgamated Industrials collapse
1923		Civil War and strikes	Northern Ireland Parliament
1924	John Murphy 1841-1924	Stained-glass commemoration	Labour Government
1925	Sir Michael III 1845-1925	2RN broadcasting plans	Hitler's *Mein Kampf*
1926	Michael Murphy Ltd. taken over by Coast Lines	Shannon Scheme	
1925-29	General strike		
1937	Joseph X.Murphy 1860-1937 T.D. 1927-32	Aer Lingus	Spanish Civil War 1936-39
1944	Owen Joseph Murphy 1904-44	'The Emergency' continues	World War 1939-45

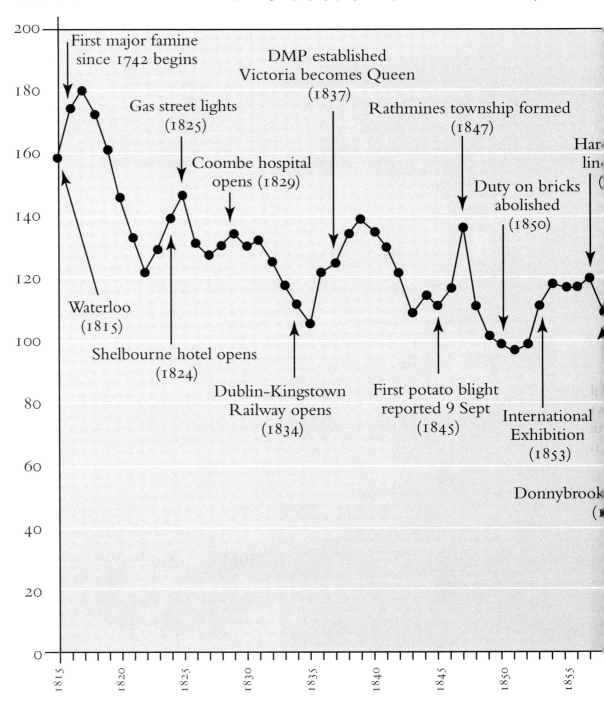

THE MOVEMENT OF PRICES, 1815–1907 (1914—100) Source: Central Bank, Tony Farmar

First major famine
since 1742 begins

DMP established
Victoria becomes Queen
(1837)

Gas street lights
(1825)

Rathmines township formed
(1847)

Coombe hospital
opens (1829)

Har
lin

Duty on bricks
abolished
(1850)

Waterloo
(1815)

Shelbourne hotel opens
(1824)

Dublin-Kingstown
Railway opens
(1834)

First potato blight
reported 9 Sept
(1845)

International
Exhibition
(1853)

Donnybrook
(

-14-

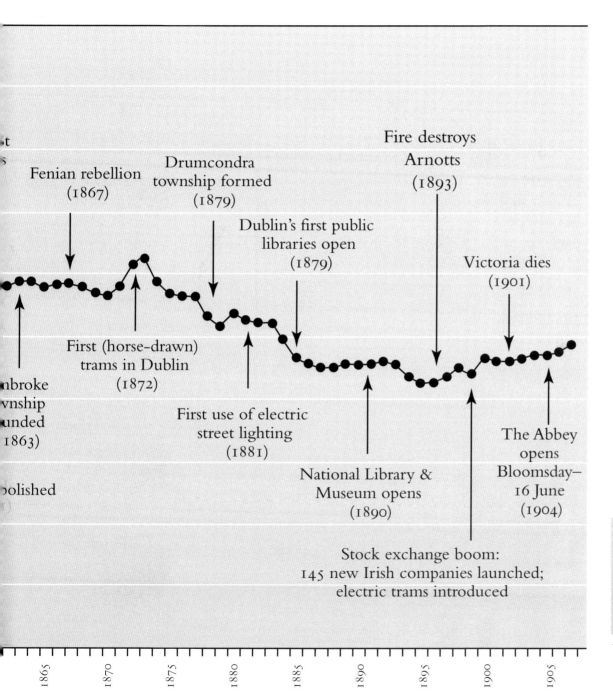

Fenian rebellion
(1867)

Drumcondra
township formed
(1879)

Dublin's first public
libraries open
(1879)

Fire destroys
Arnotts
(1893)

Victoria dies
(1901)

First (horse-drawn)
trams in Dublin
(1872)

First use of electric
street lighting
(1881)

National Library &
Museum opens
(1890)

Stock exchange boom:
145 new Irish companies launched;
electric trams introduced

The Abbey
opens
Bloomsday–
16 June
(1904)

nbroke
vnship
unded
1863)

olished

1865   1870   1875   1880   1885   1890   1895   1900   1905

C.P.I.★	1914	10
C.P.I.	1919	215
C.P.I.	1923	180
C.P.I.	2001	7,370

★ Consumer Price Index

—4—

Economic Background

River Liffey
Head sculptured by Edward
Smith
Impression courtesy Jan de Fouw

The Young Irelanders were nationalist romantics who challenged the pragmatic businessmen of the Chamber of Commerce. Mystic though he was, George Russell ('AE') (1867-1935) was a practical economic planner of international stature. He co-operated with Sir Horace Plunkett (1854-1932) in recognizing the true requirements for an economic infrastructure in Ireland.

Arthur Griffith (1871-1922), in his paper *Sinn Féin*, was the first Home Ruler to develop a serious philosophy of economic as well as cultural nationalism. His non-violent concept of economic self-sufficiency had its echoes in the Murphys' policy of having their ships built and repaired in Dublin where feasible. Griffith strove for limited tariffs to overcome Ireland's chronic underdevelopment of equity capital and entrepreneurial skills. The Murphys may have sympathized with his support for a dual monarchy, as a concession to Ulster Unionists. To digress, it is interesting to look at the subsequent history of Griffith's economic plan. In 1923 the fledgling state was faced with a world-wide slump, aggravated by the combination of de Valera and the 'Irregulars'. Griffith's policies were not feasible then. The survival plans were prudently implemented by J. J. McElligott and Robert Brennan. When de Valera did come to power in 1932, costly tariff protection was imposed. Stagnation continued until the 1960s. The Sinn Féin strategy was abandoned when Ireland voted to join the European Economic Community in 1971.

The Murphys were practical supporters of the Sinn Féin policies enunciated by Arthur Griffith and Thomas Kettle (1880-1916), Professor of Economics at University College Dublin from 1908 to 1914. From a business viewpoint, this created a conflict for them. The easy course was for them to concentrate on cheap transport of goods from the all-powerful foreign manufacturers through London, Liverpool and Hamburg for

distribution by rail to Ireland's agricultural hinterland. The Sinn Féin plan presupposed deep sea import and export facilities for Dublin-based industries. This would indeed have been a risky capital-intensive strategy. Dublin became a warehouse economy with low added-value to sustain better living conditions for its expanding population. The self-interested market economies won out over the social objectives of the common good.

The Great War of 1914-18 ended an era of British economic power. The wide fluctuations in the Consumer Price Index (CPI) after long stability in costs made business decisions unpredictable:

"The Pigeon House": a painting by William Sadler (1782-1839).
Soldiers escort a wagon towards the Military Barracks. A ship has docked. Its passengers may take themselves to Mr. Pidgeon's House for rest and refreshment. The building is now used by the E.S.B.
Courtesy National Gallery of Ireland

Burgh Quay in 1820 with the 'new' Custom House in the background.
By Henry Brocas
Courtesy National Gallery of Ireland

Will the euro confer some long-term discipline and stability to the Irish Price Index?

There was no chart of econometric projections to guide the Palgrave Murphy management in the long-term decision to renew their investment in shipping or, alternatively, to negotiate terms for the takeover of their remaining ships by Ulster Steamshipping Company or B & I / Coast Line plc.

The Quakers★ were prime movers in the commercial world of Victorian Ireland.

Their explosion of entrepreneurial energy in the eras of Henry Grattan and Queen Victoria was extraordinary. Like their Roman Catholic neighbours, the Quakers were restricted by the Penal Laws. Shrewd, frugal landowners moved naturally into becoming trustworthy wool merchants, millers and grain merchants. Brewing was then seen as an extension of the food chain. This platform of creditworthiness provided a basis for their expansion into transport by canal and railway and into importing wines, tea and coffee. Cross-channel shipping lines were established before 1800. These were followed by destinations in America and far-off China. Bewley & Webb shipbuilder's yard on Dublin's North Wall was a logical expansion of their transportation business.

The Quakers likewise contributed to the establishment of insurance in Ireland. Their merchant banking serviced the gentry as well as the traders. Members of the Quaker

Shipping at Eden Quay and George's Quay, c.1843. The photograph is attributed to the Rev. Calvert Jones and is believed to be the earliest photograph of the port of Dublin.
Courtesy National Maritime Museum, Greenwich

Arrival of the *Sirius* at New York 22 April 1838. This was the first ship to cross the Atlantic using power alone – just hours ahead of the *Great Eastern*. Captain Roberts and nearly half of the crew were Irish (including the stewardess). *Courtesy B & I Line, Hazel P. Smyth*

community were innovators in actively supporting the Royal Bank of Ireland in 1836. Like the emerging Catholic businessmen, these Quakers were not numerous in Dublin, but some were outstandingly successful in the eighteenth century. Their radical views conflicted with the conservative culture of the established Anglican Church of Ireland at that time.

Politically, many of the Quakers were more liberal than their Unionist Church of Ireland neighbours, but remained aware of their English heritage. They were more conscious of the rights of others. The outlooks of Daniel O'Connell, the Suffragists and the Pacifists were not repugnant to a free-thinking society, but appalled the conservatives.

Quakers were doubtful of the wisdom of evangelical 'Souperism' because the use of food relief as a means of religious proselytization provoked such a divisive reaction. The Quaker relief in the Great Famine survives in folk memory and has been researched by the historian Rob Goodbody.

The view down the Liffey towards the sea, with the Custom House facing a litter of merchandise and a paddle steamer *c.*1900s. *Courtesy Liam Byrne National Library of Ireland.*

Quakers with business interests similar to the Palgraves and the Murphys include:

Allen, Richard,	1803-85, competitive businessman and philanthropist.
Bewley	of Bewley & Webb, ★ Shipbuilding Yard.
Malcolmson	of Waterford, shipbuilding, iron, cotton and milling.
Penrose	Cork export – import merchants.
Pike ★	Cork Steam Packet Company.
Webb	of Bewley & Webb.
Wigham, John R.★	Engineer and improvements to lighthouse illumination.

Fellow members of the liberal Stephen's Green Club include names such as Jonathan H. Leopold, J. Tod Hunter Pim, Jonathan Hogg and Richard Grubb.

~5~

Black Gold – Coal and Steam

STEAM

Old English steam = West Frisian steam. In 1788 J. Rumsey wrote *A short Treatise on steam* whereby is clearly shown '… that steam may be applied to propel Boats or Vessels of any burden.'

The first practical steam paddle boat, the *Charlotte Dundas*, was built on the river Clyde in 1801. However, it was twenty years afterwards that Lloyd's Register mentioned these steamers. The St. George Steam Packet Company Limited★ was the first in Ireland.

COAL

Cheap coal revolutionized Victorian Dublin. Coal fuelled railways and steamships. It lit and heated homes and offices. The coal merchants and importers, such as Michael Murphy, grew rich on this ever-increasing market in post-Famine Ireland. The tonnage of coal imported through the Port of Dublin doubled between the 1860s and 1914. A man with a horse and cart could become a coal merchant. The owner/captain of a sailing collier was a ship-owner. The capital required for small-scale operations was still relatively small.

Sailing colliers carried most of the coal because, although erratic and hazardous, they were cheap to operate. In the 1860s the steam tugs gave them a new lease of life by towing them into the estuaries of the Mersey and the Liffey. During World War I freight rates quadrupled in this increasingly dangerous trade. It was steam which powered the ships and locomotives which made the ever–expanding British Empire administratively possible. This seemed important for the rising middle classes in Ireland who sought positions in the colonial services.

The hegemony of King Coal was overthrown by the revolutionary forces of oil, gas

and hydroelectricity in the 1900s. Atomic power arrived later. A successful clean air campaign finally banished King Coal and his once so highly remunerated courtiers. A modern motorship was ordered by the new Palgrave Murphy company in 1954 because steamers were no longer economic for the short sea trade.

King Coal ruled the waves in the Victorian era:

Uninhibited by the romantic traditions of sail, the Palgraves and the Murphys were quick to grasp the economics of coal and steamers.

1816	First paddle steamers introduced.	170,000
1822	Paddle steamer to Liverpool by St. George Steam Packet Company.	
1838	Captain Roberts★ from Cork in charge of *Sirius*★, the first steamer to New York.	
1851	Dublin registered ships : 377 small ships, mostly sailing colliers.	
1860	Deep-sea vessels of 1,000 tons now commonplace at Eden Quay. Steamers carried most cross-channel traffic. Steel largely replaces timber for ship-building.	
	Sailing vessels still carried coal and overseas trade.	330,000

TOP LEFT:
Typical collier brig of the 1830s discharging in the Pool of London pre-steam.
From the engraving by E.W. Cooke

TOP:
For centuries the standard unit load for grain and similar products was the sack – handled by muscle.
Courtesy Lloyd's Log

COAL IMPORTS
TONNAGE (APPROX.)

The method of discharging coal cargo remained unchanged for many years. The photograph shows dockers filling tubs in the hold of the collier and a filled tub being tipped into a railway wagon for C.I.E. *Courtesy Dublin Port & Docks Board. H. A. Gilligan.*

1860   Towage facilities for large sailing ships provided by Clyde Shipping Company, despite the wreck of two of its tugs. The Dublin Port and Docks Board purchase tugs.

1861   Safety measures introduced following disastrous gales. The Murphys must have felt an affinity for the granite obelisk erected on the east pier of Kingstown harbour. This commemorates Captain Boyd's boat and the fifteen other vessels sunk there in that gale.

1880s   Steamers compete for overseas trade. Sailing schooners still carry coastal freight.

1889-91   Seamen and dockers' strikes – unrest continued until 1914.

1897   Turbine engines, invented by Charles Parsons★ from Birr Castle, rendered existing ships' engines practically obsolete.

1900   Oil terminal opened by Esso.   100,000

1921   Oils and petrol for transport expand competition for coal. Statistical tables conceal the dangerous and ill-paid lifestyles of the collier seamen and coal porters. Cormac Lowth's researches into shipwrecks on the Dublin coastline graphically bring home to us this poignant saga.

~6~

Shipping

She starts, she moves, she seems to feel
The thrill of life along her keel,
And, spurning with her foot the ground,
With one exulting, joyous bound,
She leaps into the ocean's arms!

The Building of the Ship
HENRY WADSWORTH LONGFELLOW (1849)

The Thames (aka Argyle) – a 14 H.P paddle-steamer – was the first to call at the Port of Dublin in May 1815, just before Napoleon's Waterloo. Source B & I Line, Hazel P. Smyth

6.1 SAIL VERSUS STEAMERS AT RINGSEND THE TUGS AND THE COLLIERS

The 'Shipping Murphys' came from the Ringsend/Irishtown area where the Dodder joins the river Liffey. It was the principal port and dockland for passengers and cargoes in the seventeenth and eighteenth centuries, a role it had taken over from Dalkey.

The history of the dockland is given in McCreedy's Dublin Street Names. He mentioned Lazars' (Lepers') Hill, now Townsend Street. This is a grim reminder of the medieval plague of leprosy. A hospice was founded circa 1220 for the pilgrims to Santiago de Compostella in Spain. St. James was the patron saint of the lepers. Leprosy (Hanson's disease) in Dublin had died out by 1700 but various other skin disorders continued to be treated at this hospice.

Michael Murphy II, J.P. had various addresses in the area c.1820 as a shipping agent and coal factor. In the 1840s his address was 27 Great Brunswick (now Pearse) Street. Then came the important career move to 17 Eden Quay, beside William Barton and Charles Palgrave. Carlisle (O'Connell) Bridge and the new Custom House and Eden Quay had already been built in the 1790s. The big ships could berth there even after the original Butt swivel bridge was opened in 1879. However, Eden Quay was no longer available to shipping after 1888. In summertime the river Liffey stank! The Palgrave Murphy offices had to put up with the malodours because the main drainage scheme was delayed until 1906.

This modern port of Dublin was born with the construction of the Great Sea Wall in the 1760s and the Pigeon House★ some 30 years later. Captain Bligh's survey in 1800 provided the blueprint for the development of Dublin's harbour. The big ships sailed past Ringsend to dock at Sir John Rogerson's Quay (1728-73) and Eden Quay (1780s). The packet boats moved across to Howth Harbour in 1810. The shallow Ringsend harbour was left to the sailing fleets of fishermen, colliers, hobblers and the rowing clubs, together with the traders who continued to service them. These hobblers were the boatmen who hazardously vied with each other for employment in mooring vessels after arrival in port.

Hugh Murphy, shipwright of Sir John Rogerson's Quay, built a gabbard (barge) for the Ballast Office in 1786. No doubt he was the precursor of the famous Murphy Boatyard which survived until the 1950s. The *Ouzel Galley*, which was to provide the seed capital for Dublin Chamber of Commerce, was built in Ringsend. The Murphy Baths was another example of the name in the area.

In the eighteenth century the Dodder powered the mills for local industry. Passengers from the packet boats walked across the firm sands to travel by Ringsend over the Ball's Bridge. The frequent floods disrupted their passage to the city centre. The Grand Canal extension provided inland transport for the coal, salt, chemicals, glass and abattoir industries from 1790.

There was some employment but the Ringsend tenements were described as squalid, overcrowded and insanitary where drunkenness was rife. As late as 1869 there was an outbreak of typhus fever. Lord Fitzwilliam, who was a benevolent landlord, was criticized for the management of that part of his Pembroke Estate.

Oliver St. John Gogarty romanticized in his poem *Ringsend*:

    From inordinate wrongs,

    Imagined, outrageous

    Preposterous wrongs,

    Till peace at last comes

    Shall be all I will do,

    Where the little lamp blooms

    Like a rose in the Stew;

    And up the back garden

    The sound comes to me

    Of the lapsing, unsoilable

    Whispering sea.

The first generation of steamships had distinctively tall funnels. Gandon's masterpiece provided the backdrop, circa 1823.

H.M. Royal George was built as a 72 gun frigate in 1827. Steam, 400 H.P. engines were added later. She fired the royal salute for the Prince of Wales at Kingstown in 1868 and was paid off a year later.
Courtesy National Library of Ireland

The Murphy birthplace was a world apart from the Palgraves' salubrious north Dublin suburb.

This eighteenth-century dockland, which existed when Ringsend was a community practically independent of the city, was described by Joseph W. Hammond (Old Dublin Society 1943):

> It was the home of mariners, shipbuilders, shipbrokers, rope and sail makers, ship chandlers and outfitters as well as doctors, apothecaries, confectioners, grocers, brewers, in addition to a floating population of packet ship passengers, sailors, revenue officers, smugglers, military patrols, and press gangs for whom the many inns and taverns provided creature comforts. Fights between sailors and press gangs were commonplace as indeed were those between smugglers and revenue men, or excisemen as they were sometimes known. A fresh corpse discovered following a fracas of this kind was a prize sought after by medical students. George's Quay was the place of embarkation for prisoners being transported, in many cases for relatively minor offences, to the Virginia tobacco plantations. Following the American War of Independence, the destination of such prisoners was usually Botany Bay. There were also prison ships anchored off Ringsend or in the anchorage which later became the modern Alexandra Basin; sometimes, these prisoners were offered the choice of service in the British army or navy in return for their liberty.

Many foreigners dropped anchor in Ringsend and settled there. The Brixton fishermen from South London were influential in modernizing their industry. The formation of the Catholic parish in 1787 recognized the growing importance of Ringsend. The Church of St. Patrick was built in 1859. By then the population of Ringsend had risen to 2,064 and the number of dwellings to 190. The controversial National School was opened in 1846, too late to teach Michael Murphy II, J. P., who was by then a young man. The Technical School catering for the marine industries was not opened by Earl Fitzwilliam until 1892.

The Great Famine 1845-50 did cause poverty and disease. Presumably fishing boats and colliers provided some relief. In 1839 these fishing boats were so numerous as to impede the new-fangled paddle steamers. However, the increasing number of these cross-channel and continental ships would provide employment for deckhands and

A Ringsend fishing smack, the *Bessy*, rescued passengers from the paddle steamer the *Granuaile*, 1847.
Courtesy Edmond Symes

firemen. The Dublin Port and Docks Board was not slow to appreciate the necessity of providing steam tug facilities in 1864.

The Dublin Metropolitan Police barracks for the district was built in Irishtown. The Castle considered the Ringsend area to be disaffected. This political ethos continued on into the 1912-26 period. An 'Agin the Government' attitude may be understandable under such circumstances, but it did inhibit the commercial investment which the derelict harbour area needed so badly.

Surely this hungry, high risk, outward-looking community was a natural breeding ground for the entrepreneurial skills exhibited by Michael Murphy II, J.P.

6.2 MARINE INSURANCE – WRECKS

The merchant community which met at Mr. Edward Lloyd's Coffee House in Tower Street, London since 1688 fulfilled an economic need. It was to the coffee houses that Samuel Pepys of the Admiralty went to get shipping information. Entrepreneurial businessmen required risk capital in ever-expanding sums. Lloyd's then, as now, provided a marketplace for the spreading of risks borne by merchant shipowners. Without this

facility, the Palgrave Murphy Company could not have persuaded the Royal Bank of Ireland, supported by the Quaker community, and others to provide them with the credit necessary for the phenomenal explosion of their steamer fleet in the 1850s and 1860s. The part played by Quakers★ such as Pim, Pike, Penrose and Malcolmson in these exuberant financial services has been well described elsewhere.

From 1844 Lloyd's insurance market moved to their 'Room' in the new Royal Exchange Building in the city of London. The open informality of the coffee house was replaced by the culture and ethos of the Victorian clubs. By then there was a network of upwards of 350 Lloyd's agents throughout the Empire and beyond. They provided an unending stream of information to the Market Room. Insurance was increasingly about the scientific calculation of risk. The amateur gamblers of the coffee houses lost out. Mr. Morse's electric telegraph was installed in the Market Room in 1851.

Dublin was a part of this global communication network which was open to subscribers. They would have been the first to get information about their losses in the shipwrecks such as the *Titanic* in 1912. This was originally reported by Lloyd's List as 'down by the hull and all passengers taken off'.

During World War I, marine insurance underwriters at Lloyd's were hit hard by U-boat activity in the Atlantic. However, the government had undertaken to assume eighty

TOP LEFT:
Gale at Kingstown, 1861
Illustration: *Illustrated London News*

TOP:
The Hampton, a coal boat wrecked on the railway embankment at Salthilll in 1900. The Seapoint Martello Tower can be seen to the right of the vessel. Illustration: *Courtesy Harold Lett and Cormac Louth.*

per cent of all war risks not covered privately at uniform rates. This allowed marine insurers to offer highly competitive rates for safer voyages. The unthinkable happened when Count Zepplin's airships bombed London in 1916.

The wreck of emigrant ships such as the *Empress of Ireland* caused heavy loss of life and capital. The Dublin Port and Docks Board was developing resourses to curb this toll of the sea on the dangerous Irish coast. They co-operated with the shipping companies in safety measures such as weather forecasting, lighthouses, life boats and marine legislation.

The *Illustrated London News* graphically recorded these developments, and modern Irish historians such as Cormac Lowth at the Maritime Institute have researched the nineteenth century of tragic shipwrecks too numerous to quantify.

The schedule of Lloyd's insurance policies, dated 1913, demonstrates this management strategy. This can be compared with the professional valuation of the Palgrave Murphy fleet★ on the occasion of the death of Charles Palgrave in 1893.

The Fleet Lists laconically record some of the shipwrecks. Collisions in the busy approaches to the seaports were a constant source of claims in the pre-radar era.

Palgrave Murphy was also in business as insurance brokers and was an agent for the Liverpool Underwriters Association. The influential position of Lloyd's Agent in Dublin was established in 1812. It was held by John Walsh from 1842 to 1881. Then George Bell & Company was appointed and continued for more than a century.

The Liverpool Underwriters and Shipowners Association operated independently of Lloyd's of London from 1802 until 1845. Then the two shipping registers were amalgamated, but the Liverpool members retained special representation.

Presumably the individual Palgraves and Murphys 'joined the club' by becoming 'Names' through syndicates underwriting at Lloyd's. Their commercial expertise should have enabled them to minimize the personal unlimited liability risks involved.

The mind of Antonio as a merchant of Venice was:

> Tossing on the ocean …
> where his argosies with portly sail …
> Do overpeer the petty traffickers,
> That curtsy to them …
>
> I. 8. 13

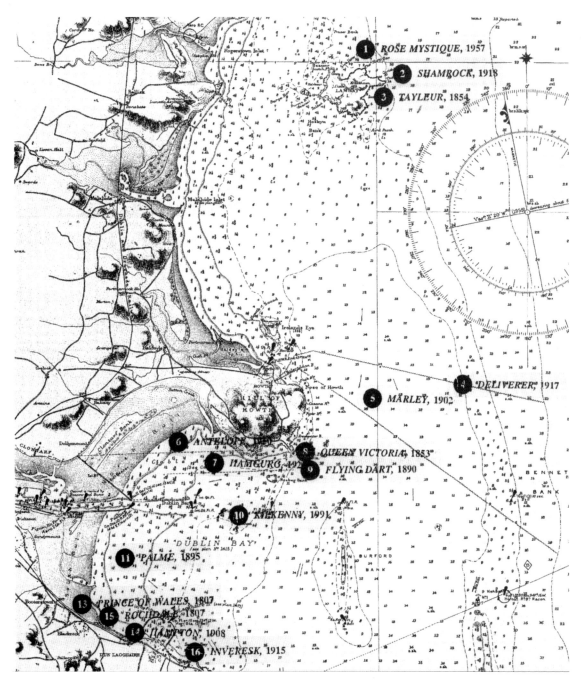

Location of vessels wrecked on the North Dublin coastline. *Courtesy* Cormac Lowth. Background details from Admiralty Chart No.1468 (1977, with soundings in fathoms).

SCHEDULE OF LLOYD'S INSURANCE POLICIES IN FEBRUARY 1913
'CITY' FLEET OF 12 STEAMSHIPS.

	Value for Insurance Hull, Machinerty etc £
City of Belfast	10,000
City of Berlin	8,000
City of Brussels	10,000
City of Cadiz	7,000
City of Cologne	8,000
City of Cork	11,000
City of Dortmund	8,000
City of Frankfurt	13,000
City of Liverpool	10,000
City of Munich	12,000
City of Oporto	10,000
City of Stockholm	15,000
Total Value for Insurance	£122,000

NOTES

1. The total premiums for the year from 17/2/1913 was about £9,000. The risks were spread across various underwriting syndicates.

2. This list may be compared with the valuation on the death of Charles Palgrave in 1893.

3. After the War★ only one venerable steamer, the *City of Munich*, was returned by H.M. Admiralty for the Murphys to plan their future business strategy.

4. No similar information is available for the steamships and sailing colliers operated by Michael Murphy Ltd. and for the Dublin General Steamship Company Ltd.

Last of the Arklow Schooners These small vessels ran regularly from Arklow to Dublin and back with general cargoes for manyyears, and formed an inexpensive method of transport. But when they became too old to be seaworthy, they were not replaced. Their russet sails and black hulls lying alongside Butt Bridge formed an attractive picture, with the Custom House across the river as a background for fifty years or more.
Courtesy Flora Mitchell and Allen Figgis

which sailed cross-channel and to Baltic and Mediterranean ports in competition with the Palgrave Murphy steamers. However, the Arklow ships were in the tramp cargo trade and thus were dependent on irregular cargoes where time of delivery was not vitally important. By the end of the nineteenth century, some Arklow vessels had auxiliary engines.

This Arklow industry provided vital services in two world wars, despite heroic losses.

BEWLEY & WEBB – SHIPBUILDING YARD. The traditional building and repair of wooden sailing vessels was carried on in Dublin docks and at Ringsend. In 1862 Thomas Walpole and William Webb★ revived steel shipbuilding in the port. Thomas Bewley★ joined the firm and later Walpole retired. The first steamship was built in 1865. In the 1890s the business declined and the dockyard was almost derelict.

In 1885 Prince Edward and Princess Alexandra opened the North Wall extension with access to the graving dock (now included in the Dublin Docklands Development).
In 1901 Scott & Smellie started the Dublin Dockyard Company.
In 1918 Woodman & Clarke of Belfast, with Bailey & Gibson of Dublin, continued the shipbuilding yard until 1928.
In 1923 the name and interests of the Dublin Dockyard Company were taken over by Vickers of Barrow in Furness until the 1937 closure.

THE BRITISH & IRISH STEAM PACKET COMPANY LTD. (referred to herein as the 'B & I' line) The history of the Palgrave Murphy Group would not be complete without a simplified record of its contemporary, the 'B & I'. *The B & I Line* by Hazel P. Smyth is a compendium of this information.

1836	B & I formed in Dublin. Its Liverpool and London ships had auxiliary steam power.
1879	B & I incorporated.
1908-14	Dublin & Glasgow S.P. Co. takes control of B & I and merge into Coast Lines Group of London.
1919	Coast Lines plc takes control of City of Dublin S.P. Co. Ltd.
1926	Coast Lines plc takes control of Michael Murphy Ltd. and Dublin General S. S. Co. Ltd.
1936	Lord Kylsant blamed for wrongful accounting in the Royal Mail case. B & I S.P. Co. (1936) Ltd. reconstituted within Coast Lines Group
1965	B & I shares bought from Coast Lines by Irish government as a semi-state enterprise.
1969-70	B & I Line operated by Limerick S. S. Co. Ltd. as part of Hibernian Transport Group until its liquidation.

| 1971 | P. & O. Line takes over Coast Lines Group, including B & I. |
| 1992 | The Irish Continental Group plc acquires the B & I Line from the Irish government. The direct sea link to the United Kingdom and France continues through Irish Ferries. |

CITY OF DUBLIN STEAM PACKET COMPANY LTD. 1822-1924

A profusion of shipping companies operated in the Port of Dublin in the nineteenth century. The Irish Sea was a stormy, high-risk area in which to survive. The line was founded by the entrepreneurial Charles Wye Williams in 1822. Four years later the ambitious company owned 15 ships, which were also active in the Mediterranean and transatlantic trades. This was in friendly association with the Peninsular & Oriental Steam Navigation Company (P & O Line) – which is, indeed, still active in the Port of Dublin.

The City of Dublin Steam Packet Company Ltd. was reconstituted in 1838 with the support of Arthur Guinness and other businessmen. The Royal Mail contract was held from 1878 to 1919, despite stormy seas and fierce competition from the London & North West★ (LNW) and the London Midland & Scottish (LMS) railway companies. The mail boats bore popular household names until 1919: *Leinster*★, *Ulster, Connaught,*

TOP LEFT:
B & I steamer terminals on North Wall quays. Note B & I shed.
Courtesy J. Brady and A. Simms

TOP:
S.S. *Wicklow*

Munster. These names were continued when the B & I took over the Liverpool and Manchester services.

However, the company was severely criticised for its treatment of Famine emigrants. It did establish a dominant position in the expanding cattle export trade.

Like the Palgrave Murphy fleet, these Kingdom ships suffered severely in the Great War. On 10 October 1918 a bereaved Dublin was shocked by the news of the sinking of the *Leinster* outside the Kish bank with a loss of more than 500 lives.

It was the loss of the Royal Mail contract to LMS in 1919 which permitted the takeover of the Liverpool & Manchester trade by the B & I Line. Historically there had been a happy relationship between the two companies, with shared directors such as Frank V. Martin and the chairmen, William Watson, and his son Sir William.

The City of Dublin Steam Packet Company Ltd. was a public company quoted on the Dublin Stock Exchange. The general meetings received full coverage in the newspapers. However, the published accounts were opaque and obscured by political intrigue. John Murphy was a shareholder and director when the company was wound up in 1924.

TOP LEFT:
Advertisements Shaw Guide
1850

TOP:
The *Ulster* of 1860. This was
one of the quartet of mail
boats, named after the four
provinces, which were specially
built to enable the City of
Dublin S.P. Co. speedily to
fulfil its obligations under its
agreement with the Admiralty
for the carrying of mail.
Courtesy B & I Line
Hazel P. Smyth

CORK STEAMSHIP COMPANY (LTD.) 1843–1927

The Cork Steamship Company and its predecessor, the St. George Steam Packet
Company (1821-43), are important in the history of steam.

In April 1822 the steam-driven, wooden-built *St. Patrick* was launched for the
Liverpool/Bristol to Dublin/Cork run. The St. George Steam Packet Company is
claimed to be the third-oldest steam shipping company in the world and the second to
operate a steamship commercially in these waters. It was a direct competitor of the
Palgrave Murphy Group.

Quaker★ entrepreneurs who were responsible for this pioneering venture included
the Pike★ family, Joseph Robinson Pim★ and Robert J. Lecky.

More technical information about the St. George Steam Packet Company is recorded
by Dr. J. M. Barry in *Queenstown for Orders : Queenstown Harbour and the Port of Cork 1800
– 1922*.

City of Cork Steam Packet Company (Ltd.) 1871-1965 was ultimately taken over by B & I / Coast Lines 1920-26.

See Biographies − Pike family and John Robinson Pim

See Quakers − Appendix 14.6

GALWAY LINE 1858-64

Variously known as the: Atlantic Steam Navigation Company, Great Ocean Steam Ship Company, and Atlantic Royal Marine Steam Navigation Company.

Timothy Collins's *Translantic Triumph & Heroic Failure* is a model of carefully researched marine history. This is an exciting story of the unlikely partnership between John Orwell Lever (1824-97), a successful Manchester shipping financier and corn miller who was elected MP for Galway in 1859 and Fr. Peter Daly (c.1790-1865), a dynamic but controversial parish priest of Bushy Park, Co. Galway − an earlier version of the late Monsignor James Horan of Knock Airport fame.

The Galway Line had some incredible successes, but came to an early liquidation owing to Atlantic storms, loss of Royal Mail contracts, the American Civil War and undercapitalization to meet international competition.

The company was a pioneer like its contemporaries William Palgrave and Michael

Murphy II, J.P. They recognised the commercial possibilities opened up by coal and steam for merchant shipping business. However, the Dublin partners were both experienced shipping brokers and developed their company successfully in a wider European market which they knew well. Michael Murphy Ltd. had transatlantic sailing cargo vessels. They did not subscribe to the Galway share issue.

HEAD LINE was owned by Ulster Steamship Company Ltd.★
The Head Line was founded by Gustavus Heyn and his son Frederick. John Gordon★ became the company's Dublin Manager. In 1917 Ulster Steamship Company took over Lord Line, followed by B & I in 1922. The Group operated ships between Belfast, Montreal and Quebec and the short sea routes to the Continent.

Ultimately the capital power of the mega Coast Lines / P & O Group made the Head Line Group shipowning enterprise unprofitable.

TOP LEFT:
Paddle-steamer *Adriatic* over-wintering in the pack ice off Cape Breton Island. Source: *Illustrated London News*

TOP:
The Man for Galway Punch cartoon of Fr. Daly offering inducements to Prime Minister Lord Palmerston, to ensure that the the postal subsidy is given to the Galway Line. Fr. Daly caused his Bishop to wish that 'someone would rid me of this troublesome priest'.

IRISH SHIPPING LTD. (1941-84)

This enterprise lies outside the 'Palgrave Murphy' era and has been well documented elsewhere.

After 1922, various Irish governments had no resources to encourage local shipowners. Irish Shipping Ltd. was a panic response by Seán Lemass to actions by the German and the Allied governments. The company continued to trade after the 'Emergency' in competition with Head Line and Ulster Steamship Company Ltd. until loss-making ventures forced it to cease trading, leading to its final liquidation in 1984. Irish Continental Group may be said to continue the traditional trading routes in competition with Stena AB.

LONDON & NORTH WESTERN RAILWAY COMPANY

The London & North Western Railway Company actively developed the railway mail services between Kingstown and Holyhead during the 1840s. Initially the company was a partner of the City of Dublin Steam Packet Company. In the 1850s a protracted conflict for the Royal Mail contract suspended this agreement until 1919 when the London Midland & Southern took over the contract.

In the 1860s the London & North Western Railway Company extended its facilities at Dublin's North Wall. Rail links were built and a hotel added.

The London Midland & Southern (LMS) took over the London & North Western Railway Company in 1921. LMS controlled most of the British ports engaged in the Irish trade.

T. & C. MARTIN

The shipping enterprises of the Martin★ family are writ large in H. A. Gilligan's *A History of the Port of Dublin*:

> The name of Martin has been associated with the timber trade in Dublin since the 1830s and the partnership of the brothers Thomas and Charles Martin commenced shipping their timber stocks from Canada in their own Canadian-built sailing ships in 1839. Another member of the Martin family, Richard (later Sir Richard Martin★, Baronet, Deputy Lieutenant and Justice of the Peace) was a member of the port authority for over thirty-six years and chairman in the years 1899, 1900 and 1901. Richard had his own timber business located at Sir John Rogerson's Quay and the

berth used for the landing of his cargoes near Cardiff Lane is still frequently referred to as 'Martin's berth', notwithstanding its official description as Berth No.5. In 1881 Richard decided to diversify his business and went into shipowning with a small sailing ship, *Lady Cairns*, 1265 tons. Between 1883 and 1892 six further vessels were acquired and the Richard Martin fleet thereby became the largest fleet of iron or steel-hulled, square-rigged ships to be registered in Dublin. These vessels carried cargoes between Europe, North and South America and Australia and the best known of them were the barques *Finglas*, *Rathdown* and *Howth* – all over 2,000 tons gross, and the smaller *Dunboyne*. The *Rathdown* was the fastest vessel in the fleet but was lost without trace in 1900. Following the death of Sir Richard Martin in 1901, the company gradually went out of shipowning, the last vessel to be sold being the *Howth* in 1910. In 1926 the company closed down and its timber trade was taken over by T. & C. Martin Ltd. which continued as a publically quoted company for another generation.

P & O LINE (PENINSULAR & ORIENTAL STEAM NAVIGATION COMPANY plc).
P & O had a long association with B & I and City of Dublin Steam Packet Company. In 1971 it took over B & I/Coast Lines. In 1975 its Pandora roll-on, roll-off enterprise would revolutionize the Port of Dublin.

SAORSTAT & CONTINENTAL STEAMSHIP COMPANY LTD.
To avoid confusion, a note on this company is helpful.

Captain Alan S. Gordon★ and his associates took over Palgrave Murphy & Company Ltd. from Coast Lines / Heyn Group in 1926. In 1934 the Saorstat subsidiary of Palgrave Murphy was formed to take over and operate the Head Line ships on their short sea routes (see Fleet Lists). These 'city' ships operated despite suffering attacks by German aircraft in World War II.

In 1969 the company merged with Limerick Steamship Company as part of the Hibernian Transport Group, which went into spectacular liquidation in 1970.

TEDCASTLE MCCORMICK & COMPANY LTD.
Robert Tedcastle had sailing colliers in 1846. The steamer *Dublin I* was built in 1866. It was converted for passengers and general cargo on the Dublin-Liverpool run in competition

with the Palgrave Murphy Group. John McCormick joined the partnership in 1897.

From 1900 onwards the crews became dissatisfied with British rule and their dangerous working conditions. Consequently they were prone to involvement in Republican gun-running activities.

Tedcastle McCormick & Company was taken over by the B & I Coast Line in 1919. In 1926 it absorbed Michael Murphy Ltd. and its associate, Dublin General Steam Shipping Company.

THE ULSTER STEAMSHIP COMPANY LIMITED
(aka The Head Line★) (aka The Lord Line)

G. HEYN & SONS (LTD.)

This Group became the most important shipping business in Ireland during the nineteenth century. The authoritative history of the Head Line by W. J. Harvey is an invaluable resource for information.

Unlike Dublin (*The Deposed Capital*), Belfast expanded phenomenally between 1860 and the Great War. Ship-building, engineering and linen were hugely profitable. The population grew from 87,000 in 1851 to 349,000 in 1901. It was not then apparent that Belfast was losing the trade war with Hamburg and the Ruhr Valley.

The 'unsinkable' *Titanic* was built by Edward Harland and Gustavus Wolff in 1912. It marked the zenith of the engineering, manufacturing and construction activities of the people of Belfast. This most appalling shipping disaster mocked the self-confidence of the whole Irish mercantile marine industry. There were still some fundamentalist bible folk who saw that iceberg as the wrath of God visited upon the followers of Darwin and Tyndall.

Ulster was the hinterland for Ulster/Head Line ships to sail to romantic-sounding ports such as Singapore, Calcutta, Bombay, Colombo, Odessa, Port Said, Las Palmas, Baltimore and New Orleans, as well as the coastal, British and Continental waters.

The 1909 Report and Statement of Accounts is included in the Accounts Appendix (14/2). At the onset of the Great War in 1914, the fleet stood at seventeen vessels totalling 51,000 tons.

G. Heyn & Sons (Ltd.) had been general merchants and ship-brokers since about 1850. In 1877 The Ulster Steamship Company Ltd., a public company registered in Dublin, took over the shipowning business. Thereafter Heyn & Sons continued as ship managers, agents, stevedores and engineers. It was incorporated in 1920 and the share capital, £100,000, was owned by the Heyn menfolk.

The important Harland & Wolff connection came about through the marriage of Gustavus Heyn to Letitia Pirrie. She was a daughter of (Viscount) William James Pirrie (1847-1924) who controlled that great shipbuilding yard. He was a Liberal Lord Mayor of Belfast in 1896/97. Her nephew (Lord) William Pirrie, went on to become chairman of Harland & Wolff and joined Lord Kylsant★ on the board of the Royal Mail Steam Packet Group.

In 1919 The Ulster Steamship Company took control of Palgrave Murphy & Company Ltd., including the 'Calcutta trade'. The *City of Munich* was transferred for £30,000 and was renamed *Wicklow Head*.

The takeover of The Ulster Steamship Company Ltd. by Amalgamated Industries Ltd. in 1920 for £2.7 million ended in receivership in 1922. E. Maloney F.C.A., of Peat Marwick Mitchell, was appointed Receiver.

G. Heyn & Sons Ltd. was appointed to manage The Ulster Steamship Company Ltd. and Coast Lines, subsequently acquiring these assets from the debenture-holders. By 1926 the Heyn Group owned 83% of the new Palgrave Murphy Limited.

That continuing history of the relationship with Coast Lines and the Heyn interests is outside the scope of this Palgrave Murphy saga. However, the biographical note on Captain Alan Gordon illustrates some more contemporary developments.

Chevalier Gustavus Heyn in Consular dress. From an oil painting in the Head Line Boardroom.
Source Head Line W. J. Harvey

THE HEYN DYNASTY

The Chevalier Gustavus Heyn (1803-75) came from Danzig to Belfast in 1825 as Consul for Prussia. He married Letitia Pirrie in 1830; a daughter of William James Pirrie. By 1850 Gustavus was a general merchant, shipbroker and acted as consul for five states. Three of his sons successfully expanded the family business:

Frederick (Fritz) L. Heyn (1850-1928) - a friend of Captain Alan Gordon★.
                                         Captain Royal County Down Golf Club 1907.
James A. M. Heyn   - Belfast
John M. Heyn   - to India and then to New Orleans Agency, 1898.
                                         Died there in 1931.

~7~

The Murphy Shipping Group

They that go down to the sea in ships,
doing business in the great waters:

The age-old business of organising merchant shipping became highly structured. By 1840 both William Palgrave and Michael Murphy II, J.P. were shipping agents. They provided trustworthy services to vessels and crews in the harbour. It was a skilful business which involved dealing with the port authority and customs and the payment of crews, repairs and marine insurance on behalf of shipowners.

After a decade or so, they became ship-brokers in a fiduciary position, negotiating the terms and conditions of charter party business deals for their principals who owned the ships. A syndicate of entrepreneurial investors could buy a vessel in the 64 shares★ as defined by the Shipping Act of 1854. These owners might delegate the practical management of their ships to ship-brokers and to agents in the ports where the ships docked.

The Murphy Shipping Group (1825-1926) is described.

The history of each company in the Group is set out separately:

Chapter 7.1   (A)   Palgrave Murphy & Company (Ltd.), including the 1893 settlement.

                     (B)   The Captains and the Crews

                     (C)   The Great War 1914-18 and the Post-War Crisis.

Chapter 7.2   (A)   Michael Murphy Limited

                     (B)   M. J. Begg & Company (Ltd.)

The biographies of the Proprietors of the Group are given:

The Murphy Shipping Group benefited from:

      (a)   Dublin's expansion 1850-1914 – Chapter 4

      (b)   new technology linking coal and steam power – Chapters 5 and 6

Dublin made the Murphy family and their fortunes.

The Tagus estuary when the first Palgrave Murphy steamers called there. Painted by Joho Pedrosa (1825-90) Courtesy Maritime Museum, Lisbon

After the Act of Union in 1800, Dublin remained the expanding administrative and transport hub of Ireland. The population of the city and its suburbs, albeit in direst poverty, expanded by one-third during this period. Shipping and the newly built railway network provided a conduit for a flood of cheap manufactured goods from Britain and Germany. This wiped out much of Dublin's manufacturing industries. However, local transporters and merchants thrived in this warehouse economy. This socio-economic history has been classically described by L. M. Cullen and Mary E. Daly.

Land transportation – Development of rival technology
The Automobile Show, organized by the (Royal) Irish Automobile Club at the Royal Dublin Society, Ballsbridge in January 1907, marked the recognition of the wider commercial importance of motor transport of people and goods. The internal combustion engine would supersede steam power. More ominous still for the hegemony of the steamship was the formation of the Aero Club of Ireland at the (Royal) Irish Automobile Club. They organized the first 'aviation meeting' at Leopardstown Racecourse in 1910.

In addition, the club opened a motor yacht group which must also have excited the Murphys at the Royal Irish Yacht Club. However their shipping enterprises did not seem to have been pioneers in any application of internal combustion lorries to transport goods from the port. A Serpollet steam car was driven by John Brown of Belfast as early as March 1896. This certainly interested the Palgrave Murphy management. Perhaps the failure of Serpollet to cope with Irish roads daunted initiative to experiment.

The Viceroys Dudley (1902-05) and Aberdeen (1905-15) were enthusiastic pioneer automobilists, but the Murphys were slow to follow their social leaders in this respect.

7.1 (A) PALGRAVE MURPHY & COMPANY (LTD.)
Ernest B. Anderson in his *Sailing Ships of Ireland* tells us that:

> The Palgraves of Dublin have a long association with the shipping world, and were engaged on the coastal trade as far back as 1828. In that year the wooden yacht *Owen Glendur* was built for them at Limington. She was a vessel of 59 tons gross, and belonged to a class of coastal craft that has long passed from the seas.

Note: The yacht was a new type of ship which originated in seventeeth-century Holland.

The Lord Lieutenant of Ireland, Lord Aberdeen, at the wheel of his Daimler, leaving the 1907 Dublin Horse Show. Lord Grenfell, Commander-in-Chief of the Crown forces in Ireland, is seated beside him.
Courtesy RIAC Archive

The word yacht means hunter or fast vessel. It was designed for seamen in the Dutch inland waterways and then became a standard type of small coastal cargo ship. The yacht was then adapted for leisure purposes.

M. Murphy Junr., and W. Murphy of College Green owned a few sailing vessels for a time.

The first of Palgrave Murphy's fleet of 'City' boats was built in 1862. She was the *City of Cadiz*, a screw steamer of 785 tons, rigged as a three-masted schooner, and built by Richardson, Duck & Company of Stockton. She was followed in 1864 by *City of Lisbon*, built by Langley, and *City of Dortmund* in 1865, another Richardson, Duck vessel.

By 1885 a fleet of twelve vessels had been acquired and services were maintained to Hamburg, Bremen, Ghent, Antwerp, Amsterdam, Rotterdam and the North American ports. As these ships were all more or less standard pattern screw-propelled vessels of 700 to 1,200 tons register, I will not deal with them here.

The Morways of the Sea proposal by the European Union would serve these same traditional trade routes.

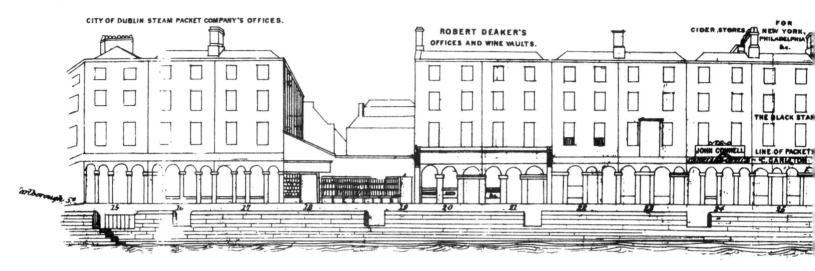

CITY OF DUBLIN STEAM PACKET COMPANY'S OFFICES.

ROBERT DEAKER'S OFFICES AND WINE VAULTS.

CIDER STORES

FOR NEW YORK, PHILADELPHIA &c.

THE BLACK STAR

JOHN CONNELL

LINE OF PACKETS

Capital Requirements

How did this unlikely, but happy, shipping partnership of these Palgraves from Great Yarmouth and Michael Murphy II, J.P. from Ringsend develop so rapidly during the post-Famine 1850s?

The shipping business suddenly became more capital-intensive with the development of the paddle-steamer during the Industrial Revolution. The Palgrave connection would have made an expanding business credit worthy in the eyes of ship-builders and bankers. The establishment of a London office added status in the international shipping business, as did Charles Palgrave's move there. No doubt Michael Murphy II, J.P. provided an intimate working knowledge of the labour and practices obtaining in the Port of Dublin.

Merchant ships were traditionally operated by syndicates. The vessel was owned by investors in 64 parts or shares. The working capital could be financed separately by the trading parties. The cargoes were commonly owned by importing merchants. This long-established mercantile financing operation continued to evolve in sophistication. The whole high-risk business could be underwritten through Lloyd's of London.

In post-Great War Dublin the comfortable Murphys had no competitive urge left to compete against the ruthless Greek shipping families and the major international shipping corporations.

Beresford Place

The 1893 Settlement

Charles George Palgrave died in London on 26 May 1893. He had retired to England in the 1850s. Presumably he directed the office in London which was still the great international hub of mercantile trade and enterprise. This death was a watershed for the Murphy family because of his half-share in the partnership with Michael Murphy II, J.P., who was to die in the following year, aged seventy-eight.

The legal position had been established by the beautifully worded draughtsman of the Partnership Act of 1890 with its lucid English composition which has been a model for parliamentary draughtsmen ever since. This Act simplified the decisions for the Executors, Paine, Ouchterlony and Woodhouse in London, and for the Murphy family. In the event, this important takeover was negotiated by these businessmen expeditiously and pragmatically. The Palgrave Murphy business would not be broken up and sold off. They level-headedly avoided the legal route through the Chancery Court in London. Perhaps Charles Dickens's great contemporary classic *Bleak House*, with its vigorous satire on the abuses of the Chancery Court in the case of *Jarndyce and Jarndyce*, influenced the decision for a businessman's practical solution.

The thirteen steamships were professionally valued on the basis of age and tonnage (see Appendix 14.8). The half-share of goodwill was finally agreed at only £2,187. The

agreed formula used was apparently calculated on a simple average of net profits for five years: £6,623 p.a. less one-third divided by two.

The deal was done and the consideration of £20,000 was paid over within the year retrospectively to 31 May 1892.

The litigiously minded children of Edward Smith★ (1807-88), colliery owner of Liverpool, and the Bellamont Estate in County Cavan, would contest their differences through the Chancery Court for twenty-one years at an unbelievable cost and frustration.

The way was clear for the brothers John, (Sir) James and (Sir) Michael to continue Palgrave Murphy & Company (Limited – incorporated in 1911) and to co-ordinate their still expanding general shipping and coal businesses. They appear to have adopted a policy of buying second-hand ships. Perhaps this was influenced by a shortage of capital after the demise of the old partnership. It may, however, have been caused by the desire for greater personal drawings to pay for a more affluent lifestyle. They were in a position to know about the conflicting warlike policies of the German and British Empires, but no one could have foreseen the economic consequences of the Great War of 1914-18.

Agreement – Executors of Charles Palgrave – died 22 May 1893
and Michael Murphy II, J.P.
Operative from 1 June 1893
The Schedule hereinbefore referred to

Name of Steamer	Number of shares held by Charles George Palgrave
Minerva	24 sixty-fourths
City of Cadiz	28 sixty-fourths
City of Lisbon	28 sixty-fourths
City of Dortmund	26 sixty-fourths
City of Cork	28 sixty-fourths
City of Liverpool	24 sixty-fourths
City of Malaga	28 sixty-fourths
City of Oporto	24 sixty-fourths
City of Belfast	24 sixty-fourths
City of Amsterdam	28 sixty-fourths
City of Hamburg	22 sixty-fourths
City of Bristol	24 sixty-fourths
City of Rotterdam	24 sixty-fourths

Under the Act for the Registering of British Vessels 1825, the property in every ship or vessel of which there is more than one owner was to be divided into sixty-four parts or shares. When a ship was first registered, the new owners took an oath required by this Act declaring the number of shares held. However, the subsequent changes in beneficial ownership are less easy to trace.

7.1 (B) THE CAPTAINS AND THE CREWS
Skilful research by David Snook, based on official archives and census returns in Britain and Ireland, revealed a linkage between the traditional seafaring families of Rush and Skerries and the Palgrave Murphy Group. After 1830, the small farmers and fishermen found employment on the merchant ships serving the expanding cross-channel ports, such as Liverpool, Bristol and Glasgow. The leading seamen adapted to change and

became master mariners. They might well give preference to local men when selecting a crew. Farm labourers could go to sea as firemen.

Palgrave Murphy & Co. was a major employer of seamen from Rush, County Dublin, in the twenty years before 1914. In 1914 Rush men comprised a quarter of the 240 seamen employed, mostly as seamen or deck officers, rather than as engineers or firemen. It must have been a lonely, dangerous and harsh livelihood. The wages were acceptable compared with labouring work. Probably there was some chance of a little smuggling as a sideline. It was hard labour for deckhands and stokers, with uncomfortable quarters and rough food from the galley.

The crews had some clubhouse facilities provided for them by religious groups. In 1856 the Church of Ireland Mission to Seamen was opened at 13 Eden Quay, Dublin. This was rebuilt after the bombardment in Easter week 1916. The port continued to shift downstream, so the Mission moved to Alexandra Basin in 1984.

The Stella Maris Seafarers' Club was opened at Sir John Rogerson's Quay in 1910 by the Society of St. Vincent de Paul. In 1962 the club moved to 3 Beresford Place, which is at the rear of the Custom House.

Thomas Hoare (born 1856) was a master mariner who worked for Palgrave Murphy between the 1880s and 1913. The casing over the drive for the wheel is marked 'Hamburg'. *City of Hamburg* was built new in 1881 for Palgrave Murphy.

The photograph may have been taken around that time and may be of *City of Hamburg*. Man on left in cap looks like the Captain. Man on right looks better dressed. Women or girls on left and right look as if they could be sisters and middle class.
Courtesy Captain Hoare's family and David Snooks

The Cargoes

These small steamers were scheduled to sail as a regular service rather than as 'tramps'. General cargo was carried as and when it could be obtained through local agents.

The German names of the 'City' ships in 1914 indicated the growing importance of cargoes between the thriving manufacturing hinterland of the ports of Hamburg, Glasgow, Bristol, Cardiff and Newport, as well as their home port of Dublin. There was a contract with Arthur Guinness to carry dried grain to Hamburg and Rotterdam. Bowater paper for the *Irish Independent* was carried from Rotterdam. Flour, potatoes and sugar also featured. These exports of surplus sugar resulted from the successful sugar beet cultivation innovated by Count Otto von Bismarck in the 1850s. A cargo of Welsh coal to Lisbon might be combined with a back load, including wine and fruit.

The 1,000-mile voyage from Dublin to Hamburg would take around five days at eight knots. A ship on this run would expect to return to Dublin every three weeks. For older men with families, this was a more attractive option than working the North Atlantic where a man could be away for months.

'Die Englander holen ihr Mittagessen' – *Die Woche*, Berlin, September 11, 1915. Ruhleben prisoners on their way to a midday meal. *Courtesy J. D Ketchum*

I must down to the seas again, to the vagrant gypsy life,
To the gull's way and the whale's way where the wind's like a whetted knife;
And all I ask is a merry yarn from a laughing fellow-rover,
And quiet sleep and a sweet dream when the long trick's over.

JOHN MASEFIELD, *Sea Fever*

7.1 (C) THE GREAT WAR AND THE POST-WAR CRISIS

World War I altered fundamentally the economic and social world for Dublin-based ship-owners. The dreadful crisis had been no secret, yet the call-up of Reservists on 3 August 1914 shocked all who worked in the Port of Dublin. Suddenly the demand for maritime skills soared. There was a surge of business for the Dublin dockers at Alexandra Basin. Reluctant steam trawlers were commandeered for dangerous armed patrol and mine-sweeping action.

The German government immediately seized five Palgrave Murphy ships in Hamburg (see Fleet Lists). A further three ships were sunk (see Schedule B).

Schedule A

Name	Built	Bought	
City of Berlin	1874	1897	Sunk as a blockship 1915
City of Cadiz	1862	1876	Returned and sold 1919
City of Belfast	1876	1889	Returned and sold 1919
City of Hamburg	1881	1881	Returned and sold 1919
City of Munich	1879	1907	Sold to Ulster Steamship Co. May 1919 for £30,500

The British Admiralty likewise seized German ships, which were then auctioned in December 1914. Fortunes were there to be made for a few wealthy ship-owners who could foresee four years of submarine war at sea. Arklow owners did purchase three of these ships.

There had been ample forewarning that Britain would not remain neutral, so it is surprising that so many of their ships were caught in German ports. It appears that German port authorities exercised their powers some days before 4 August 1914. The crews were interned first at Hamburg, together with other Irish merchant-men from Arklow and elsewhere.

Since their employers had no legal obligation to continue to pay wages, the men were penniless until the British government arranged an allowance. They were then transferred to Ruhleben ('Peaceful Life') prison camp. This was on the racecourse in the Berlin suburb of Spandau. The scene there was carefully recorded by J. D. Ketchum, a Canadian music student, who was aged twenty in 1914.

Initially, living conditions were reasonable under the circumstances. However the camp was congested, insanitary, cold and dark. Most of the 1,300 seafarers were housed in Barracks 8 and 9. This did reduce their stress of loneliness and boredom. Father Schmidt from South Africa volunteered to remain on at Ruhleben.

The Irish theatrical group could stage plays by Synge and Shaw and by the prisoners themselves. However from 1917 onwards, all civilians in Germany suffered severely from the increasingly successful blockade by the Allies, which was in answer to unrestricted submarine warfare. The International Red Cross negotiated the exchange of some of the

HMS Helga in Dun Laoghaire 1916. Note the guns mounted fore and aft and the addition of barricades along the main deck to give some protection from snipers (*George Montgomery*).

sailors in the year before the Armistice was signed on 11 November 1918.

In Dublin the military occupied the North Wall extension and the Bull Wall. All merchant ships came under government control 'for the duration'. Rear Admiral Evelyn Merchant commanded the Dublin Bay area and availed of the organizational skills of David Barry★ and other civilian executives.

The sight of the *Helga* gunboat shelling O'Connell Street in 1916 must have seemed ominous.

Three ships had been sunk by the Germans:

Schedule B

City of Berlin   seized – sunk as blockship 1915 – per Schedule A.

City of Bremen,   Tonnage 1258 Gross, Built 1899
4.4.1915: Torpedoed and sunk in the Atlantic 20 miles S.3/4 W. from Wolf Rock by the German submarine U24 while on a voyage from Port Talbot to Bordeaux with a cargo of coal. Four lost.

City of Swansea   Ex Gwendoline, Tonnage 1375 Gross, Built 1882
25.9.1917: Torpedoed and sunk in the English Channel 15 miles E.N.E. from Betty Head by the German submarine U40 while on a voyage from Tyne to France with a cargo of coal. Two lost.

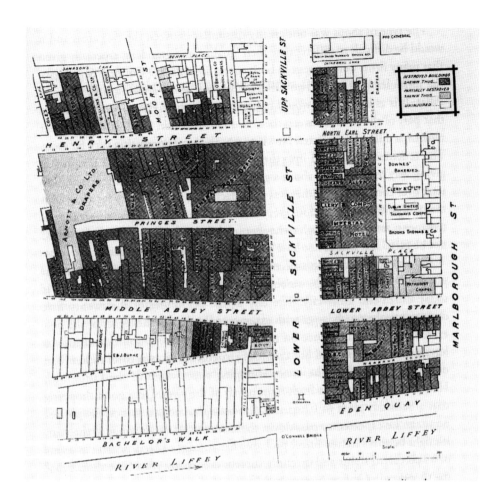

The destruction of 1916 is shown on Goad Fire Insurance Plan. The darker shading shows buildings destroyed, the lighter shading shows those partially destroyed.
Courtesy Joseph Brady

Almost all Lower Sackville Street was destroyed, as was most of the block enclosed by Middle Abbey Street, Henry Street and Liffey Street. Much of the right-hand side of Upper Sackville Street, including the Gresham Hotel, was destroyed during the Civil War.

As the Great War ended, the takeover by the Heyn/Ulster Steamship Group continued, despite the hiccough of the collapse of Amalgamated Industrials Ltd. 1920-22. This is described in excellent detail in the *Head Line* by W. J. Harvey. By February 1926 the Heyn family owned 83% of Palgrave Murphy & Co. Ltd. Discussions were held with Palgrave Murphy & Co. Dublin, and Hudig & Veder N.V., Rotterdam, with a view to a working partnership for the development of trade between the Netherlands and Ireland. These talks resulted in an agreement.

Subsequently Captain Alan S. Gordon's★ consortium took over Palgrave Murphy Ltd.

In December 1919 the *City of Munich*, now renamed *Wicklow Head*, resumed the Belfast, Dublin and Hamburg service after five years. Also about this time the Ulster

Steamship Co. Ltd. took over the Calcutta service operated pre-war by Palgrave Murphy & Co. Dublin. Further talks were entered into with Palgrave Murphy & Co. Dublin, regarding their trade between Belfast, Dublin and Hamburg, with the view to the Head Line taking over their interests. After protracted negotiations, it was agreed that, from 11 February 1920, the Head Line would acquire the trade from Palgrave Murphy & Co. for a trial two-year period. In return, they would pay a royalty of one shilling per ton on all cargo carried. As trade developed, a few Palgrave Murphy ships were used to supplement sailings.

The Palgrave Murphy fleet (see Fleet Lists) was finally disposed of between 1914 and 1919.

				SHIPS
Ships seized by the German government – per Schedule A				5
Ships sunk by torpedoes – per Schedule B				2
In 1917/18 Palgrave Murphy had already sold five ships:				5
Name	Built	Bought		
City of Liverpool	1872	1892		
City of Brussels	1876	1899		
City of Stockholm	1882	1900		
City of Cork	1880	1908		
City of Cologne	1881	1918		
Other ships sold were:				3
Name	Built	Bought	Sold	
City of Malaga	?	1873	1915	
City of Dortmund	1865	?	1921	
City of Frankfurt	1895	1913	1921	
Total Palgrave Murphy fleet August 1914				15

The price of £30,000 negotiated with the Ulster Steamship Company in 1919 for the *City of Munich* appeared very satisfactory in view of the declining market.

To the political turmoil was added financial uncertainties, augmented by the

Dubedat★ and other scandals. Death Duties had to be provided for. An austerity policy of ploughing back profits (now reduced by Corporation Tax and Income Tax) would certainly have curtailed the comfortable lifestyles of the Murphy families. The Excess Profits Duty of 1917 at 80%, which was not repealed until 1921, augmented the gloomy forebodings of venture capitalists.

The collapse of the City of Dublin Steam Packet Company in 1919 had added to the worries of Dublin ship-owners. In April 1922 the 'Irregulars' disrupted the port by occupying the Ballast Office. Then the Pro-Treaty army took over amidst continuing sniper fire. As ever, labour disputes continued to disturb the prospect for capital investment. The old adage 'the time to invest in property is when the blood is running in the gutters' would have seemed to them to be foolhardy in the extreme!

TOP LEFT:
Custom House after the 1921 fire.

Crepe-de-Chine frocks trimmed val lace. Colours, ivory, sky, flesh and almond. Also in taffetas trimmed net. Georgette frocks over Jap silk with lace and French flowers.
These shocking ladies' dresses seemed like harbingers of chaos in the economy.
Source: Slyne's advertisement in *Irish Sketch* 1927.

Post-War Crisis

Nineteen-nineteen saw a hectic post-war boom, which lasted for two years, but this was followed by a deep slump. Joseph X. Murphy had difficult decisions to make, as did his cousin Sir George Murphy of Michael Murphy Ltd. However, they must have become increasingly aware that the renewal of their aging steamers was a necessary long-term requirement. Presumably some of these ships had been modernized and re-engined before 1914. When the Great War finally tore their world apart, their fleet was old and effectively obsolete. The small Murphy businesses could no longer compete against their wealthy British conglomerates.

The freight rates for ships requisitioned by the British government were very low. This, combined with rising costs and high taxation, impoverished the shipping industry. Palgrave Murphy was prudent to sell off elderly ships between 1915 and 1920 and to enter into negotiations with Heyn, Ulster Shipping, Captain Gordon and the B & I Line.

7.2 (A) MICHAEL MURPHY LIMITED

Hazel P. Smyth tells us about this coal-importing business which was established in the 1870s by (Sir) Michael Murphy III (1845-1925) under the name or style of Michael Murphy Junior, with offices at 37 College Green. William Murphy★ was an early associate there, but little is known about him. He may have been a master mariner. Alternatively there was a William Murphy, shipowner, also with an office at College Green in the 1870s.

As the youngest of three sons, Michael III apparently considered that his enterprise could expand as an independent entity outside the Palgrave Murphy partnership. It developed into a successful business carrying bulk coal from the Bristol Channel to Dublin and Cork. The expansion of the railways network between the 1840s and 1860s provided a market for Michael Murphy's coal and also enabled him to distribute his goods nationwide

The Murphys had a few sailing ships for a time. They had one brigantine, James, 137 tons, for a number of years and the big full-rigged ship, *Westminster*, 1,426 tons, which carried timber across the Atlantic during the 1880s under the command of Captain M. E. Morris. She was later superseded on this route by the American built full-rigger *Saint Joseph*, 1,138 tons, and by 1890 this was their only sailing vessel. The 1895 Register★ shows that the *Saint Joseph* was managed and owned by a William Murphy.

The steamers in the fleet were:

Anglian		*Ferga*	
Arthur	– named after his son	*Finola*	– Dublin built
Beatrice	– named after his daughter	*Foyle*	– named after his son
Borthwick		*George*	
Captain Cook		*Grania*	
Captain McClintock		*Ierne* or *Irene*	
Captain McClure		*Llandaff*	
Captain McClure (II)		*Patricia*	
Captain Parry		*Patricia II*	– Dublin built
Defence		*Rhona*	– Dublin built
Enda	– Dublin built	*Rosaleen (Ita)*	– Dublin built
Enda II			

The Murphy steamers had black funnels; the house-flag was red, with two white diamonds bearing the letters 'M.M.' in black. The registered manager was James O'Dowd of 3 Beresford Place, Dublin.

Notes: Ownership of Steamers per Register. See also Fleet Lists

SHARES

Captain McClintock 67771 Dublin 1876	Michael Murphy John Murphy Jas Murphy Michael Kelly John Kelly (corn merchants of Grand Canal Harbour, Dublin)	32 8 8 8 $\frac{8}{64}$	Vessel lost off Point Lynas, Orkney 9 December 1886
Captain McClure I 72648 Edw.Lindsay, Newcastle 1876, Dublin 1876	Michael Murphy Jnr.	64	Foundered off Smalls Lighthouse, Bristol Channel 4 March 1884
Captain Cook 58783 Wellington Quay 1873 Dublin 1873	Michael Murphy Jnr. Insurance Broker	64	Re-engined by Richardson, Hartlepool 1879. Wrecked at Clogher Head, 18 Feb.1899
Captain Parry 67800 Stockton 1877 Dublin 11/5/1877	Michael Murphy Jnr.	64	Vessel foundered 14 December 1893 in Irish Sea.

c.1880	Michael Murphy III established the Dublin Steamship Company as a parallel general business. Both companies moved to larger premises at the Spencer Dock and Sir John Rogerson's Quay.
1886	These businesses moved to new premises at 94 North Wall where there was good storage space and modern equipment, screens, siding, steam cranes and a patent fuel mill.
1887	Michael Murphy III expanded his general cargo business. A shipping agent such as Michael J. Begg of Cardiff became necessary. Welsh coal was an important cargo.
1894	On the death of Michael Murphy II, J.P., the word Junior was dropped from the company's name.
1905	A limited liability company was incorporated, with W. A. Frew as Secretary. It took over the business of steamship proprietors of Michael Murphy at Dublin, Cardiff and Swansea. This still operated separately from the Palgrave Murphy Company with new premises at 3 Beresford Place and 18 D'Olier Street. There were depots at 9 Bute Street, Cardiff and at Victoria Wharf, Swansea. Following the Sinn Féin economic policy, the company would build five ships in Dublin.
1919	B & I/Coast Lines took over Liverpool and Manchester trade of Palgrave Murphy. Heyn/Head Line★ would take over Palgrave Murphy & Company Ltd.
1925	Sir Michael Murphy III died on 30 June 1925, aged eighty.
1926	B & I/Coast Lines★ took over both Michael Murphy Limited and its associate, the Dublin General Steam Shipping Company, after prolonged negotiations. The business became integrated into the B & I. Sir George Murphy★ remained as a director and shareholder.
1971	P & O took over Coast Lines.
1973	Coast Lines was absorbed by Tedcastle McCormack when Coal Distributors Ltd. was founded, with unified bulk coal discharge installation facilities at the new Ringsend Quay.

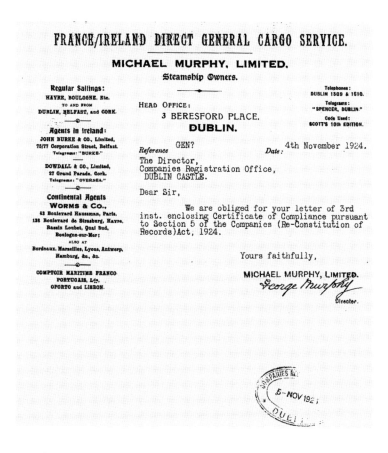

The Irish Register of Joint Stock Companies was in the Custom House where it was destroyed on 25 May 1921.

Michael Murphy Ltd. reconstitued the Company Registrar's file after destruction in 1921.

Directors	Shareholdings @ £10 each	Other Directorships
Sir Michael Murphy – British	5,998	Dublin General S.S. Co.
Governing Managing Director		M. J. Begg
George Murphy – British	2,971	M. J. Begg
Joseph O'Dowd – British	31	Manager, Ml. Murphy Ltd
		Director M. J. Begg and
		Dublin General S.S. Co.
Secretary: Edward Bowles	—	—
3 Beresford Place		
	9,000	

In 1926 Sir Alfred Henry Read represented B & I Steam Packet Company Ltd. after the takeover.

In December 1936 Liquidators were appointed:

Robert Stanley Stokes F.C.A. of Stokes Bros & Pim (established 1876)

at 36 College Green, Dublin and E. Jones, Old Jewry, E.C.2, London.

A new company took over the assets of Michael Murphy Ltd. in voluntary liquidation.

7.2 (B) M. J. BEGG & COMPANY (LTD.)

was founded in Cardiff in 1890 as shipping agents. Exports of Welsh coal became an important cargo business.

1900	Incorporated. Took over the existing business of Michael Joseph Begg, Ship Broker.		
	He held	474	shares
	(Sir) Michael Murphy III	10	
	Sundry	6	
	Issued Shares	490	
	Directors: Michael J. Begg	– resigned afterwards but retained his shares for several years	
	(Sir) Michael Murphy III	– of 88 Merrion Square	
	1907 Arthur Murphy	– of 88 Merrion Square	
	George Murphy	– of 88 Merrion Square	
	John O'Dowd	– of 3 Beresford Place	
	and John Tierney	– also served as Director	
1908	M. J. Begg & Company Ltd. availed of the facilities of the Companies Consolidation Act.		
1917	*Shareholdings*:		
	Michael Murphy Ltd.	468	
	Sir Michael Murphy of Wyckham	10	Died 1925
	(Sir) George Murphy★ of Hawthorn, Shrewsbury Road	5	Died 1936
	Arthur Murphy	5	Died 1919
	Four others	12	
	Total	500	

1919	Arthur Murphy died – shares to Sir Michael.
1920 – May	Liquidator appointed. He gave consent for a new company to be incorporated with the same name.
1921 – Jan.	Final winding up.
1926	B & I (Coast Lines) took control, together with Michael Murphy Ltd. and Dublin General Steam Ship Company. Sir George Murphy remained as a director and shareholder.

For reasons that are unknown, some Murphy ships were registered in Wales.

7.3 DUBLIN GENERAL STEAM SHIPPING COMPANY LTD.

This firm was established by (Sir) Michael Murphy III, circa 1880, in parallel with his coal-importing business, which was then known as *Michael Murphy Junior*. Presumably he thought it was better to have a separate entity for his expansion into the general shipping trade outside the Palgrave Murphy partnership agreement for profit-sharing.

1880	The offices were at 37 College Green. Premises were taken at Spencer Dock and Sir John Rogerson's Quay where there was good storage space and equipment.
1886	Moved to 94 North Wall.
1897	Agencies for general cargo in Liverpool, Swansea and Cardiff (see M. J. Begg & Co. Ltd. agency).
1905	Incorporated as limited company at 3 Beresford Place. Became associated with the Palgrave Murphy Group but still operated separately from Palgrave Murphy & Company Ltd.
1926	
7 Sept.	Taken over by Coast Lines / B & I, but continued to trade under its own name.
1971	P & O took over Coast Lines.
1973	Dublin General Steam Shipping Company Ltd. was absorbed with Tedcastle McCormack & Company when Coal Distributors Ltd. was founded.

Accountancy is a part of the 'noosphere' or 'mind layer' of conscious communication described by Teilhard de Chardin (1897-1991), the palaeontologist theologian in *The Phenomenon of Man*. Our thinking has evolved to describe the evolution of the world around us which de Chardin described as the 'biosphere'. Cardinal de Lubac (1887-91) could describe the same continuity. The accounting techniques developed by the Palgrave Murphy Company can thus be perceived as grains of sand on the shores of this evolving noosphere.

In 1696 S. Ammonet, a French Huguenot, published in Dublin his somewhat inadequate *Key of knowledge for all merchants*. However by 1807 Paul Deighnan had published in Dublin his *Complete Treatise on bookkeeping*. This might well have been a useful handbook for progressive shipping agents like William Palgrave and Michael Murphy I.

Contemporary financial statements can provide only an odd squint at the Ireland which existed in the century up to 1922. Indeed, there is little trace of further development in the techniques and philosophy of accountancy until the economic recovery of the 1850s and 1860s. Personal privacy was accepted as a citizen's right, which even H.M. Revenue Commissioners had limited power or willingness to penetrate until the Irish Free State officials exercised their newly founded authority. Financial journalists reverentially accepted financial statements on their face value. The hand-made private ledgers and minute books with their brass locks were kept in the safe. Only the senior males of the family ever saw this holy of holies.

Yet by the time Charles Palgrave and Michael Murphy II had died, Hollerith had proved the practical application of his tabulating machine in America. This would develop into International Business Machines Inc. A new accounting era had dawned.

Abstracts from the private ledger are included in Appendix 14/2. The 1909 Report of the Ulster Steamship Co. Ltd. is also given by way of contrast. However, the arcane lack of disclosure in the published financial statements of the City of Dublin Steam Packet Co. Ltd. provoked some ineffectual protest at the Annual General Meetings.

All transactions were recorded in sterling since Britannia ruled the exchanges. Bills of Exchange were already obsolete. There was a bursar on each ship who managed the various European currencies through the local agent. After each voyage the Murphys examined the Captain's statutory logbook. No doubt the bursar's journal and scrapbook were produced for scrutiny.

The busy accounts department of Harland & Wolff* in the main counting house at Queen's Island around 1912. Note high desks and rigid dress code.
Courtesy Harland & Wolff.

In 1914 the weekly wages recorded were:

First Engineer	£4 – 4 – 0
First Mate	£3 – 0 – 0
Bursar/Steward	£1 –17– 0
Seamen	£1 –15 – 0

Ships chandlers at the ports of call may have given commission to influential officers.

The importance of internal control over such diverse transactions all over Western Europe and beyond can be appreciated in the light of modern financial scandals.

Some of the Palgrave Murphy accounting procedures for recording shipping assets and profit & loss accounts, although accurate, are occasionally difficult to follow. The ships were owned separately in different shares. The primary management objective was to control the detailed profit and loss for each voyage for the private information of the partners.

Those calligraphic nominal accounts were closed off by journal entries to the half-yearly profit & loss account in the private ledger. The resultant summary became a statement of trading profit or loss, but the format of the balance sheet remained incoherent. Who designed this sophisticated accounting system? Perhaps it was based on some known precedent with which the Craig Gardner partners were familiar.

The accounts were prepared by Craig Gardner & Company, which signed the certificate after John Murphy, as partner responsible for office management, and (Sir) James. (Sir) Michael III did not sign at that time. The practice of preparing accounts twice-yearly remained the practice until the Companies (Consolidation) Act of 1908 provided statutory support for a more standardized reporting of accounting statements.

The close relationship with the accountancy firm of Craig Gardner & Company was established and involved monthly visits. This may have served to establish credit-worthiness. It was also desirable when Charles Palgrave moved away to England in the 1850s.

The names of some of the partners who, like their contemporaries Stokes Brothers & Pim, are part of Dublin's financial history.

Sir Robert Gardner	(1838-1920) 1865-1917	J.P., First President of Institute of Chartered Accountants in Ireland in 1888.
David Telford	(1850-1943) 1890-1943	President of Institute 1915-17 Liquidator City of Dublin S.P. Co. Director Royal Bank and other companies.
John Gardner	(1864-1926) 1890-1924	A signatory to the Charter in 1888. He retired to set up his own practice with John Donnelly (Senior) in 1924.
George Hill Tulloch	(1873-1957) 1910-54	A Scotsman, Director of Bank of Ireland.

Praise is due to the Craig Gardner Liquidator of Palgrave Murphy & Company Ltd., who deposited the private ledgers and papers in the Irish National Archives.

It is perhaps understandable that (Sir) Michael Murphy III should seek separate accounting services when he set up his own business in the 1870s. He went to John M.

Kean F.C.A., J.P. (1841–1908), an alumnus of the Catholic University, who commenced practice with Edward Kevans in 1874.

Later the 'Shipping Murphys' were co-directors, with Lord Kylsant, on the B.& I Board. Clive de Paula's views on Reserve Accounting, as defined in the famous leading case, were still relevant for the Irish Institute of Chartered Accountants syllabus in 1942.

Like their contemporaries, the Murphys were slow to accept the practical benefits of limited liability. This concept was brought into United Kingdom law in 1855. Far-seeing as ever, Grattan's Irish Parliament introduced the Anonymous Partnership Act in 1781 but Irish businessmen preferred to continue with the simple structure of the Partnership Act 1890 with which they were familiar. It was a classic of lucid draughtsmanship which did stand the test of time.

Banks relied on established names with reputations for credit worthiness and probity, backed by mortgaged property, rather than on independently monitored financial statements and cash flow projections. The Irish banking crisis of the 1880s demonstrated the necessity for more sophisticated techniques. As modern Irish-based multi-nationals rediscover, financial control of a diverse business requires state-of-the-art accounting control.

—8—

Politics

As the Palgrave Murphy international shipping enterprises expanded, politics must always have been prominent on their agenda. Consular appointments were useful for foreign information and status. Michael Murphy II, J.P. became vice-consul for the Grand Duchy of Oldenburg in Saxony and Italy. Sir James had the significant and important consulate for the Imperial German Empire. John was consul for Belgium.

The absence of a French connection is surprising. Likewise, the direct involvement in transatlantic shipping did not develop, despite the fact that, as shipping brokers and agents in the 1840s and 1850s, Palgrave Murphy must have been involved in arranging passages for emigrants to America. Yet this connection did not develop.

Dublin Castle increasingly gave a business importance to political trends emanating from Westminster. Hence the Murphys' selection of liberal clubs. At home, the strong political trends had a more direct impact on management decisions. Home Rule seemed conservative when confronted with Fenianism. The Irish Republican Brotherhood was allied with radically socialist trade unionism. The Murphys strove to protect the needs of business freely to control its own affairs against enactments from Dublin Corporation, as well as from Her Majesty's parliament. Regulations enacted in Westminster would control the impoverished economy. This inhibited the accumulation of the working capital necessary for growth.

Thou shalt not muzzle the ox that treadeth out thy corn on the floor
Deuteronomy XXV.4 St. Paul Epistles: *2 Corinthians 9.9* 1 Timothy 5.18

Probably the Murphys and the Anglo-Irish Palgraves with their Whig background could differ politically on O'Connell's Repeal campaign, but both remained loyal to their Queen. The middle-class Home Rulers continued to support the monarchy as a stabilizing force against partition. In Dublin there were huge popular displays of loyalty to the Crown during the visit of the Duke and Duchess of York in 1897 and Queen Victoria herself finally in 1900. T. M. Healy M.P. (1855-1931) echoed Edmund Burke when he prophetically castigated the House of Commons: '…the glories of your jingo statesmen. Is this wisdom? By what means do you hope to keep the Empire you have?'

Whether or not the British Empire did more good than harm, the twin threads of trade and capital which held it together did benefit Irish business.

George V was the last British monarch to visit Dublin, in 1911, amid scenes of great enthusiasm. There were lavish and ornate decorations along the route from Kingstown harbour through Monkstown and Blackrock to College Green. Republicans and dissident trade unionists were in a minority still.

A social historian can analyse and deconstruct the lives and myths of these Murphys, Palgraves and their associates. Their certainties and traditional approaches to economics, nationality and religions may not seem to make sense in modern terms. However their heartfelt struggles should command our sympathetic understanding, even in the facile light of retrospection.

8.1 THE DUBLIN CORPORATION VERSUS:

> The Dublin Chamber of Commerce
> The Dublin Port & Docks Board
>   and the Vice-Regal Administration

When William Palgrave II arrived in Dublin circa 1825, he encountered a city still hide-bound by a mediaeval guild system dating back to the twelfth century. The great Guild of Merchants regulated all commercial interests and was influential in politics. Palgrave might have applied for membership of the picturesque Mariners, Vintners, Ship Carpenters and Salmon-takers Guild. However, his name does not appear in the Roll of Freemen of the City. More likely his sympathies would lie with the progressive Dublin Chamber of Commerce, formed in 1783.

The guilds did not grant their considerable prestige and freedoms to non-conformists, much less to their Catholic neighbours. Catholic Emancipation was

A typical nineteenth-century Dublin slum – Poole Street off Pimlico, with the washing hanging out.

followed by the Municipal Reform Act of 1840 which brought seven centuries of patronage and pageantry to an end.

There was a power struggle at the Dublin Municipal Corporation during the nineteenth century and beyond. The capital city was the location for administration, finance and industry, but it also housed the working classes. The 1840 Act shifted control towards the largely Catholic Nationalists. It would be hard to improve on Mary E. Daly's classic *Dublin, the Deposed Capital* for a description of this evolution.

Catholic businessmen like the Murphys seem to have become alienated from the oft-times corrupt demography of the Council. They seemed to avoid national politics and increasingly to concentrate on supporting their own organizations at the Chamber of Commerce and the Port and Docks Board. This brought them into conflict with the increasingly power-hungry demagogic Corporation.

Responsibility was avoided by moving out to the newly developed salubrious suburbs administered by the Urban District Councils where *Rerum Novarum*★ seemed remote from their real world. Thus by 1900 the increasingly impoverished Dublin Municipal Corporation found itself without power against the Crown administration and those newly autonomous middle-class townships such as Pembroke, Blackrock,★ Kingstown, and Rathmines. Even the Dublin Port and Docks Board remained outside the control of the City.

The Chamber of Commerce complained of high city rates, deplorable sanitation and the continuous unrest engendered by low wages and slum dwellings. The Dublin Corporation would remain a powerless forum for populist nationalism, frustration and corruption until after 1922. *Rerum Novarum* fell on stony ground and Dublin's slums remained notorious in the civilized world.

Tennyson's diatribe was brutally explicit but might well have been applied to Dublin:

> Is it well that while we range with Science, glorying in the Time,
> City children soak and blacken soul and sense in city slime?
>
> There among the glooming alleys Progress halts on palsied feet,
> Crime and hunger cast our maidens by the thousand on the street.
>
> There the Master scrimps his haggard sempstress of her daily bread,
> There a single sordid attic holds the living and the dead.
>
> There the smouldering fire of fever creeps across the rotted floor,
> And the crowded couch of incest in the warrens of the poor.
>
> TENNYSON, *Locksley Hall Sixty Years After*, 1842

However slum tenement property could be a profitable investment. Many Councillors were personally involved in that business. Although the Dublin Stock Exchange had been established under 'Grattan's Parliament', opportunity for the investment of private savings remained limited.

FOLLOWING PAGE
Historic Dublin Guilds,
Fifteenth century. The
Mariners and Ship Carpenters
were oddly grouped with the
Salmon-takers and Vintners.
*Courtesy Mary Clark and
Raymond Refaussé*

8.2 DUBLIN CHAMBER OF COMMERCE

The early history of the Chamber is perceptively described in Professor Louis M. Cullen's classic *Princes & Pirates* (1983). Until long after the Famine, Catholics and Quakers had little influence.

The Guinnesses and the Conservatives remained in effective control until the mid-1870s. Despite the decline in indigenous manufacturing, there was expansion in transport, wholesale imports and, of course, the alcohol business. This produced a demand for a more representative council. A change of the guard was forced through. John and (Sir) James Murphy became influential in working for a more effective protection of commercial interests generally against strong action by old-fashioned governments and new-fangled local politics at home. The Chamber and the Dublin Port and Docks Board generally achieved a harmonious relationship, but a dispute about harbour dues proved surprisingly acrimonious.

There was solid support for William Martin Murphy★ and the shipping interests in the defeat of Larkin's 1913★ strike.

World War I★ was profitable for Dublin on the whole and was widely supported with enthusiasm, but conscription was another matter entirely! Home Rule then divided the Chamber.

The Murphys had a long history of support for the Chamber of Commerce during the period from 1865 to 1923.

		Year of admission	President
John	(1841-1924)	1865	
Sir James	(1842-1922)	1865	1903-04
Sir Michael III	(1847-1925)	1873	
Michael II, J.P.	(1818-94)	1881	1891-93
C.J	Committee	1909	
G.V.	Committee	1909	
E.F.	Committee	1916	
J.P.	Committee	1918	
Joseph X	Committee	1922	
(Sir) George Francis	Committee	1923	

8.3 THE DUBLIN PORT & DOCKS BOARD

While the Chamber of Commerce represented the interests of the wider business community, the Dublin Port and Docks Board was a more focused professional association. Henry A. Gilligan's *History of the Port of Dublin* (1988) authoritatively describes this vital channel for overseas trading in the pre-aviation days. The colourful times of the Ballast Office and John Pidgeon's house lead on to the establishment of the Port Authority.

> *Charles Dickens lauds a magnificent city:*
> Traveller, pause upon Carlisle Bridge and gaze on the stately Custom House, the ships too few, alas! – and the great port of Dublin. All lie eastward, and eastward too, stretch more quays, lined chiefly with shipping and bonding warehouses, and shops for the sale of ships' stores.
>
> (*Household Words* 1853, p. 586}

Carving of the *Ouzel Galley* on the Chamber of Commerce building, Dame Street, Dublin. The merchant ship *Ouzel Galley* set sail from Ringsend in 1695 and was eventually presumed lost. She reappeared in 1700, laden with pirate loot. The city merchants set up an independent arbitration committee to resolve the conflicting claims. This successful organization was the precursor of Dublin Chamber of Commerce. *Courtesy Bord Fáilte*

Merchant's Hall and Arch,
Wellington Quay Built by
Merchant Tailors' Guild
1821.
*Courtesy Mary Clark and
Raymond Refausse*

The seals of the
Corporation for preserving
and improving the port
of Dublin and of the
Dublin Port and Docks
Board which succeeded it
as the statutory authority
for the port in 1867.

The expansive Victorian period from 1830 until 1880 provided the space for the Palgrave & Murphy family enterprises to operate. The hugely capital-intensive programmes built up the facilities necessary for steamships to load and discharge at the city quays. The Grand Canal docks had been there since 1796. The seventeenth-century Harbour Master's house survives amidst the Irish Financial Services Centre developments. However, the huge Custom House Dock, opened by King George IV in 1821, was demolished in 1927.

On the north side, Stack A was designed by John Rennie in 1820/21. No doubt the Palgraves and Murphys witnessed the famous 'Crimean Banquet' there in 1856 since their offices were on Eden Quay, which was still used by shipping until after the opening of Butt Bridge in 1879. Stack A is being preserved as a classic example of Victorian commercial architecture within the Irish Financial Services Centre development. Hardwicke, the property group founded by the Dublin businessman Michael F. Judd (1861-1932), plays a leading role in this renewal of the Port and Docks area in modern times.

In 1860 another new graving dock, designed by William Dargan, gave facilities for repairs to larger ships. The Alexandra Basin is still in use. Inspired by a self-confident spirit of enterprise, expenditure continued on dredging, quay walls, berthing facilities, cranes and railways – all made economically feasible by the new-fangled power of the steam engine. The Board's loans, which helped to finance these capital expenditures, were quoted on the Stock Exchange.

Steam Tugs

The first steam packet company had operated between Howth and Holyhead as far back as 1816. These modern paddle boats moved quickly into providing tug boat facilities for the sailing ships and colliers moving up the river towards Eden Quay.

Salvage assistance became available. The changing tides and sandbanks combined with the rocks to make the approach to the port notoriously lethal for those wooden sailing ships and colliers. Indeed, the tug boats which served them were frequently wrecked as well. While steam did provide a further lease of life, it spelt the end for sail in commercial transportation. The poor old colliers struggled on to their bitter end.

Like the Palgraves and the Murphys, the Dublin Port and Docks Board was not slow

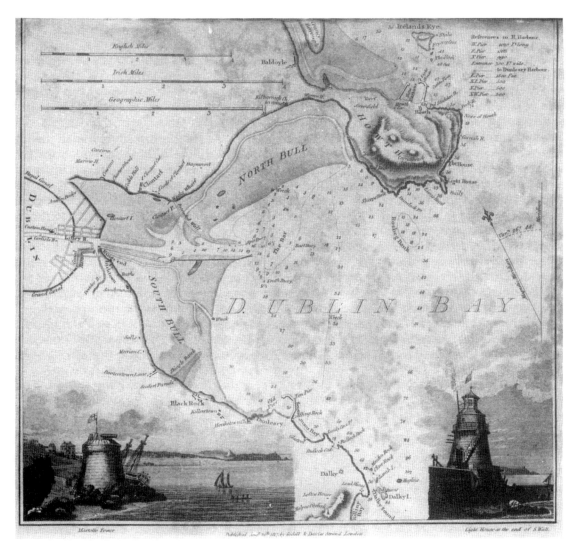

By the time of this map, 1817, the South Wall was completed. The 'Intended Wall' shown on the north side had been proposed by several people, including Bligh, with variations. The wall as finally built in the early 1920s was designed by the Ballast Board's engineer, George Halpin.★ *Courtesy* Book of the Liffey *Elizabeth Healy (Wolfhound Press)*

in reacting to this changing technology. The advantages of using a steam tug for towing the dredging floats had been demonstrated during the short-term hire of a tug in bad weather, and in June 1864 the Board accepted the tender of Grendon & Co. for the building of a steam tug for the dredging fleet. Pending delivery of the new tug, the Port Engineer, Bindon Blood Stoney,★ was authorised to hire a local tug. The new tug arrived in 1864 and by the following March Stoney reported that the new system had proved highly efficient and had justified the outlay involved.

The Launch of *The City of Dublin* lifeboat. Courtesy: *Around and About the Custom House*, Jane Meredith

The Royal National Lifeboat Institution took over from the Dublin Port Authority in 1862

Towage of ships was provided by independent operators. Competition between the towage companies was so keen that the tugs used their maximum speed to get out to the bay when a large sailing ship was reported. The 'races' caused problems for other vessels whether proceeding on the river or berthed at the quays because of the wash raised by the tugs. The 1902 Act empowered the Board to operate a public towage service, but this right was invoked only when the tugs were not engaged in towing the Board's own vessels. The private operators eventually withdrew and, following the purchase in 1916 of a small tug capable of handling the dredging plant in normal conditions, the tugs *Anna Liffey* and *Majestic* were put on public towage full-time.

The increased number and size of steamships arriving at the port provided plenty of work since large vessels, sailing or otherwise, need the assistance of tugs when navigating in confined waters such as river channels and harbours. Whereas ships of 400 tons had been regarded as large in relation to the port of Dublin in the 1830s and 1840s, deep sea vessels of 1,000 tons were commonplace in 1866.

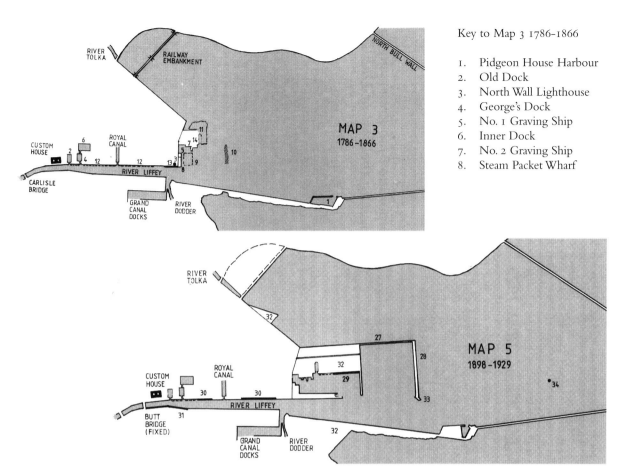

Key to Map 3 1786-1866

1. Pidgeon House Harbour
2. Old Dock
3. North Wall Lighthouse
4. George's Dock
5. No. 1 Graving Ship
6. Inner Dock
7. No. 2 Graving Ship
8. Steam Packet Wharf
9. Halpin's pond
10. 'Island' Breakwater
11. No. 1 Graving Dock
12. Timber wharves, North Quays
13. North Quays – rebuilding
14. Dockyard

Key to Map 5 1929

27. Tolka Quay
28. Eastern Breakwater
29. Alexandra Quay
30. North Quays – rebuilding
31. South Quays – rebuilding
32. Reclaimed lands
33. Eastern Breakwater Lighthouse
34. North Bank Lighthouse (new)

Courtesy History of Port of Dublin *H.A. Gilligan*

In 1868 a newly constituted Board consisted of:

Reconstituted Board 1899

Lord Mayor and 3 appointees	4	7
Irish Lights	7	Nil
Elected by traders and manufacturers	7	12
Elected by shipowners, including Michael Murphy II, J.P. (Chair, 1903)	7	9
Members of Board	25	including Murphys:

James

John

Michael III

28

Dublin Port ceased to expand after the 1880s, while its rival, Belfast, thrived on its industrial hinterland.

The Board was deeply involved in the turbulent 1913-23 decade which included the strikes, world and civil wars, to be followed by economic stagnation. In April 1916 it was shocked to see *H.M.S. Helga* sail up the Liffey and to watch salvoes being fired at Boland's Bakery, Dublin Distillery and Liberty Hall. This vessel was built in Dublin as the Irish maritime research ship *Helga II*. In 2002 a new marine research vessel, *The Celtic Explorer*, would cost €31 million.

8.4 THE IRISH STEAM SHIP ASSOCIATION

This association came into existence at No. 3 North Wall in 1851 under the chairmanship of Joseph Pike.★ Cartels are by their very nature both shy and fascinating. The ship-owners were no exception. Their records remain sketchy. Clearly there was a need for companies such as Palgrave Murphy to have their private 'club' to co-ordinate their own affairs. It did not need a prophet to foretell that competition can easily become self-destructive in capital-intensive industries. However, such associations are extremely difficult to self-regulate. There was some conflict of interest for the increasingly powerful English railway companies. Common Law has always been hostile

An aerial view of the Custom House and Custom House docks area prior to its development as the Irish Financial Services Centre. *Courtesy I.F.S.C.*

to trade protection as being contrary to the perceived good of free competition and against any monopolistic fixing of prices and conditions.

The Dublin shipping rates conference seems to have been a parallel organization.

Local manufacturing and wholesaling were damaged by the competitive fixing of through rates to provincial Irish towns. These became cheaper than Dublin's own transporters and merchants. Representations were made to the vice-regal commission in 1908 by politicians and other traders claiming extortionate freight rates.

There was an agreement between Palgrave Murphy and the Bristol Steam Navigation Company Ltd. to pool the Hamburg trade with the British and Irish ports.

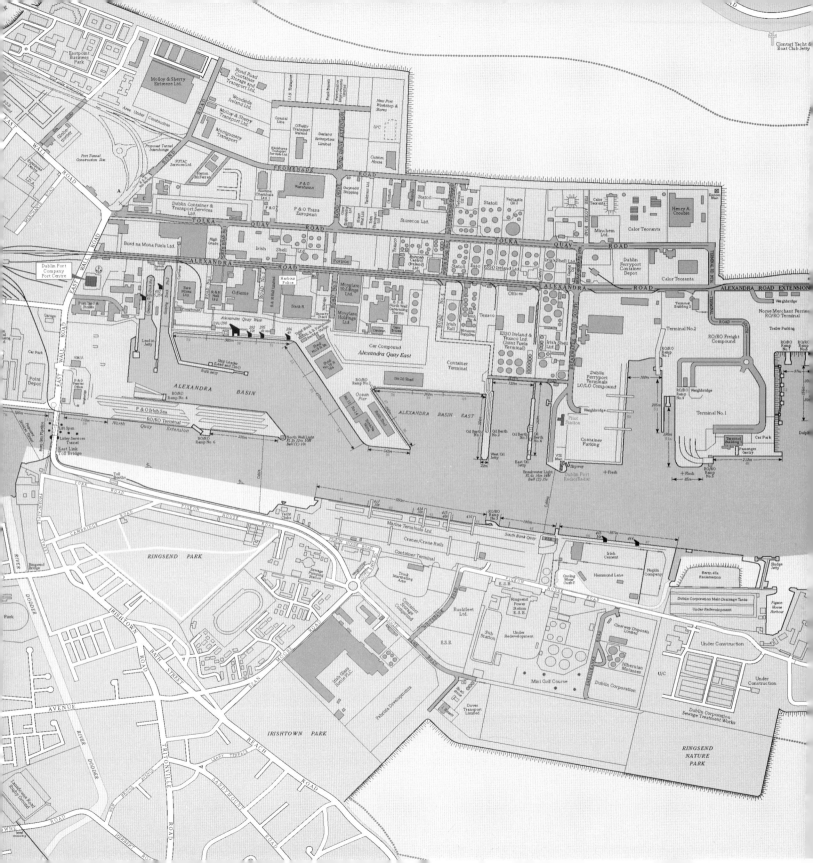

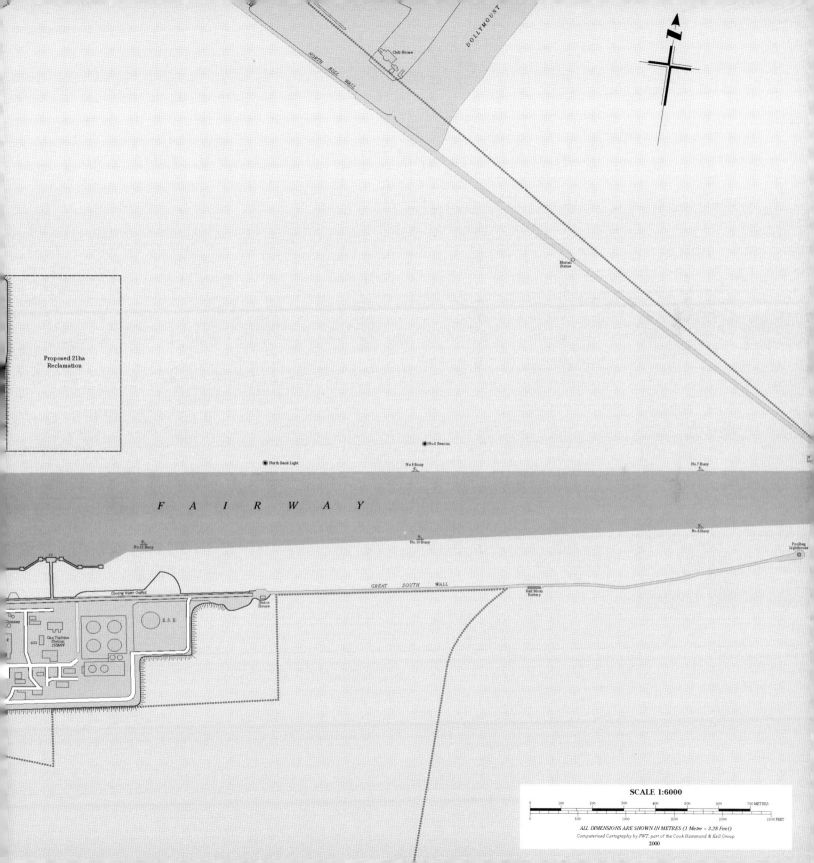

DOLLYMOUNT

Club House

NORTH BULL WALL

Marian
Statue

Proposed 21ha
Reclamation

No.5 Beacon

North Bank Light

No.9 Buoy

No.7 Buoy

No.11 Buoy

F A I R W A Y

No.10 Buoy

No.8 Buoy

Poolbeg
Lighthouse

Cooling Water Outfall

Sluice
House

GREAT SOUTH WALL

Half Moon
Battery

Chimney

Gas Turbine
Station
155MW

E. S. B.

SCALE 1:6000

0   100   200   300   400   500   600   700 METRES

0   500   1000   1500   2000   2500 FEET

ALL DIMENSIONS ARE SHOWN IN METRES (1 Metre = 3.28 Feet)
Computerised Cartography by FWT, part of the Cook Hammond & Kell Group
2000

~9~

The Vice-regal Court and the Castle in Irish Society

Arthur Vicars, Ulster king-at-arms in his ceremonial tabard. He was dismissed in 1908 following the theft of the 'Irish Crown Jewels', and subsequently was murdered in 1921.
Courtesy National Library of Ireland

Sir James Murphy was created a Baronet of the United Kingdom by Letters Patent in 1903, having become a Knight in the previous year. Sir Michael Murphy III followed him in 1912. Their brother John was not on the Honours Lists. Apparently he did not seek it or perhaps was not favoured by His Excellency's advisors. Their father, Michael II,★ was proud of his title of Justice of the Peace.

In 1912 Sir Michael III took a further step in the ritual. He employed Sir Neville R. Wilkinson, Knight Commander of the Royal Victorian Order, J.P. (1869-1940), of Mount Merrion, to assign impressive Armorial Ensigns. Sir Neville, who married a daughter of Sydney Herbert, had succeeded the hapless Sir Arthur Vicars as Ulster King of Arms and principal Herald of all Ireland. This was in 1908 after the scandalous theft of the Insignia of the Order of St. Patrick, commonly called the Irish Crown Jewels. The title of Baronet of the United Kingdom is a much sought-after British dignity. Although it is not part of the Peerage, it takes precedence over the Orders of Knighthood. Importantly the Letters Patent conferred this title on to the grantees' legitimate male heirs.

The social presumptions of this Honours system may be laughed at, but who was then to know that the Victorian British Empire was already crumbling or that King Coal would be dethroned by oil power as the source of world energy.

The Vice-regal Court and its Irish Honours★ list favoured the rising middle class. Firstly lawyers and doctors were admitted, then successful businessmen, provided they all professed allegiance to the Crown. Home Rulers who supported the supremacy of the Westminster Parliament were increasingly favoured. Being a landowner or a member of

(LEFT) Correctly dressed for the levee at Dublin Castle. Courtesy Michael Tutty, Old Dublin Society

By the 1880s formal events ot the Castle were overcrowded, extravagant displays, affirmations of position and important marriage markets. The court suit was standardized by an official pamphlet, published in 1898, *Dress Worn by Gentlemen at Her Majesty's Court*. It was then stipulated that gentlemen not in uniform were obliged to wear a 'civil uniform' of black (or very dark blue) velvet, or a dark colour cloth suit composed of coat and breeches; a waistcoat of similar fabric or in white; black silk stockings, black shoes with gilt, silver or steel buckles; formal sword with cut-steel embellishments and cut-steel buttons on the coat. Its eighteenth-century origin can be seen in the inclusion of a cocked hat, wig bag, lace frills and ruffles. *Courtesy Mairead Dunleavy*

the Church of Ireland was no longer necessary. The King's New Year's Honours List was prepared by his Prime Minister and published after Christmas with smiling faces of those newly ennobled. Most Honours were reserved for public servants and Members of Parliament. Mounted orderlies might be seen around Merrion Square delivering the much sought after invitations to the more intimate Vice-regal functions.

Imagine the excitement when the tin trunks containing the costly ordinary and full dress uniforms were delivered from the court outfitter. The full dress court suit with its golden epaulettes was finery indeed! Did contemporary Dublin businessmen, such as Sir

Queen Alexandra as Princess of Wales c.1890. Princess Alexandra charmed most of the Irish with her beauty and refreshing energies. As a pioneer photographer, she visited Lafayette for the portrait. *Courtesy Lafayette*

The opening in 1913 of the Children's Pavilion at Peamount Tuberculosis Sanitorium: Herbert H. Asquith between the children, the Aberdeens at the foot of the steps. *Courtesy: Fred E. Dixon* Asquith (1852-1928), Prime Minister 1908-16, was a Gladstonian Home Ruler. He backed down during the 'Curragh Incident' March 1914 but was compassionate in Easter 1916.

James and Sir Michael, ever learn how to wear the ceremonial sword and cocked hat in the manor born?

Despite the fact that he was in liturgical mourning for Pope Leo XIII, Dr. Walsh, the Catholic Archbishop of Dublin, attended the levee held in honour of Edward VII in 1903. The extrovert Dr. Walsh was given precedence over his Protestant counterpart. Honours became more freely bestowed than elsewhere in the United Kingdom until the system ended after the Great War. Indeed, many non-Unionists, such as William Martin Murphy★, William Dargan★ and William B. Yeats,★ let it be known that they had turned down an honour. The corrupt sale of titles developed by Lloyd George debased the honours system. Honest George V was constitutionally powerless to halt the rot.

Daisy Fingall (1866-1964), née Burke, enjoyed the Dublin season as a trend-setting Catholic aristocrat. Her husband, Arthur James Francis Plunkett, 11th Earl of Fingall, complained about Dublin as the 'city of the dreadful (k)nights'.

Sir Henry Robinson remembered the dry Dublin wit:

There they go, there they go – with their microbes and crown jules an' all
SIR HENRY ROBINSON'S, *Memoirs*

THE RIVAL HURDY-GURDYS.

MISS ERIN. "Go away, please, gentlemen; this noise is awful. If you expect me to pay you for discord, you're quite mistaken. When you've practised a little harmony you can call round again."

Alex Findlater's valuable family history throws an interesting sidelight on the role of the Vice-regal Court from their traditional viewpoint, which was insulated from their Catholic neighbours.

Administration of Ireland 1850-1922

The forceful agitation for land reform and Home Rule caused successive British governments to change their policy towards Ireland. The generous Wyndham's Land Act of 1903 was part of the plan to 'kill Home Rule by kindness'. More important administrative functions were given to the Irish Civil Service, based in Dublin Castle. Valuable government contracts and appointments were there to be distributed to His Majesty's loyal subjects. It was this locally based Civil Service which provided the administrative structure which enabled the fledgling democracy of the Irish Free State to survive after 1922.

TOP LEFT:
The Rival Hurdy-Gurdys Miss Erin – 'go away, please, gentlemen; this noise is awful. If you expect me to pay you for discord, you're quite mistaken. When you've practiced a little harmony, you can call round again'.

TOP:
The administration was bedeviled by the growing movement towards self-government.

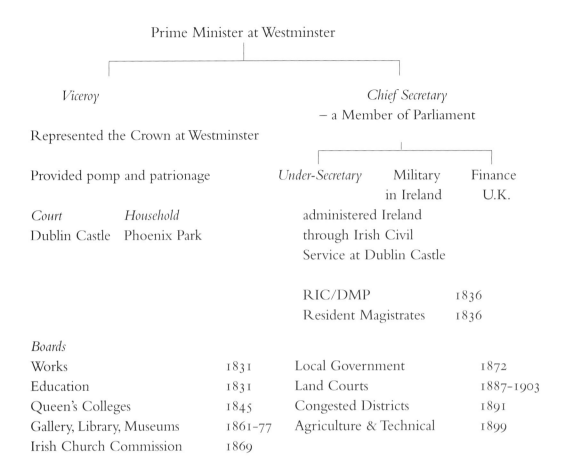

Prime Minister at Westminster

Viceroy | Chief Secretary
– a Member of Parliament

Represented the Crown at Westminster

Provided pomp and patronage | *Under-Secretary* Military Finance
in Ireland U.K.

Court *Household* | administered Ireland
Dublin Castle Phoenix Park | through Irish Civil
Service at Dublin Castle

RIC/DMP 1836
Resident Magistrates 1836

Boards
Works 1831 Local Government 1872
Education 1831 Land Courts 1887-1903
Queen's Colleges 1845 Congested Districts 1891
Gallery, Library, Museums 1861-77 Agriculture & Technical 1899
Irish Church Commission 1869

Date of Visit	1903 July	1904 July	1907 July	1911 July
King	Edward VII & Alexandra	Edward VII	Edward VII	George V & Mary
Government	Conservative	Conservative	Liberal/Home Rule	Liberal/Home Rule
Chief Secretary at Westminster	Wyndham	Wyndham	Bryce	Birrell
Under – Secretary Dublin Castle	McDonnell	McDonnell	Dougherty	Dougherty
Lord Lieutenant	Earl Dudley	Earl Dudley	Earl of Aberdeen & Ishbel	Earl of Aberdeen & Ishbel
Appointment Dates	Aug.1902 to Dec. 1905		Dec. 1905 to Feb. 1915	

Note: Queen Victoria disliked the Irish and did not visit her Irish Kingdom between 1858 and 1900. However, her son King Edward VII, as Prince of Wales, had been a popular visitor to Dublin including:

The Stephen's Green Club and the Hibernian United Services Club were joined in celebration for the visits of King Edward VII in 1903 and 1907.

1849   Aged six, with his parents.

1861   His ten months' army service at the Curragh Camp included the affair with an actress. This scandal was successfully hushed up by his shocked mother.

1865   Dublin exhibition at Earlsfort Terrace.

1868   With Princess Alexandra.

1900   With Queen Victoria on her last visit – previously in 1849, 1853, and 1861.

Cavendish, Lord Frederick (1836-82) was sensationally assassinated by the Fenians in the Phoenix Park in 1882. He was a Liberal Whig Member of Parliament. His wife was a niece of Mrs. William Gladstone, the wife of the Prime Minister.

Lord Frederick's older brother was Spencer Compton Cavendish, Marquis of Hartington (1833-1908) – afterwards the 8th Duke of Devonshire. He was a worthy Liberal Chief Secretary for Ireland (1871-74). The huge Devonshire estates in Lismore, Co. Waterford and in England made the family the wealthiest and possibly the most influential in the United Kingdom. 'Harty Hartington' was a life-long friend of both the raffish Prince of Wales (King Edward VII, 1901-10) and William Gladstone.

This political murder of the Chief Secretary and his Irish Under-Secretary Thomas H. Burke in the Phoenix Park forced both Gladstone and Parnell to rethink their plans for land reform and Home Rule for Ireland. It must also have shaken the confidence of Michael Murphy II and Sir James at the Dublin Chamber of Commerce.

Strikes and Rerum Novarum

Leo XIII. *Rerum Novarum*
Popular representations of
the nineteenth-century
popes became a devotional
feature of even the poorest
Catholic households.
*Courtesy Museo del
Risorgimento, Milan*

In the 1830s Under-Secretary Drummond had preached to the largely Protestant Landlords: 'Property has its duties as well as its rights.' Now in 1891 Pope Leo XIII used the papacy's newly re-established prestige to preach *Rerum Novarum's* avant-garde socialism to Dublin's rising generation of Catholic businessmen. Theirs was a most turbulent era not only politically but also in art, religion and economics.

William Walsh★, Archbishop of Dublin from 1885 to 1921, was slow to condemn Larkin and Connolly until the scheme to send children of strikers to England caused a hysterical outcry. The parish priest of the combined parish of Booterstown and Blackrock, Monsignor O'Donnell, had some difficult thinking to do when preaching to his socially diverse congregations.

James Larkin and his Irish Transport & General Workers Union developed the sympathetic strikes as a politically powerful weapon. William Martin Murphy★ accepted the *Rerum Novarum* teaching that trade unions and strikes were morally acceptable, but the use of widespread strikes for political ends was revolutionary and had to be resisted.

The Chamber of Commerce considered that it was Larkin who had called an illegitimate strike on that Tuesday 26 August 1913, being the first day of the Dublin Horse Show week. However, Larkin claimed at the subsequent Asquith inquiry that it was a lock-out by William Martin Murphy of the Tramway Company.

Papal teaching on social justice was still in transition at that time. 'Hard to Port' (left) ordered the captain of the barque of St. Peter in 1891, but the passengers and crew hardly heard or understood the altered course which he directed. Eamon Duffy's *History of the Popes* describes the situation perceptively :

Rerum Novarum opens with an eloquent evocation of the plight of the poor in industrial society, in which 'a small number of very rich men have been able to lay upon the teeming masses of the labouring poor a yoke which is very little better than slavery itself'. From this misery socialism offers an illusory release, fomenting class hatred and denying the right to private property. Defending this right to ownership, the Pope argues that class and inequality are perennial features of society, but need not lead to warfare. The rich have a duty to help the poor, and this duty goes beyond mere charity. Christianity is concerned with the healing of society as well as of individual souls, and in that healing the state must play a part. The state depends on the labouring poor for its prosperity and must therefore protect the rights of labour, both spiritual and material. This protection extends to regulating working conditions, and ensuring that all receive a living wage, which will allow the worker to save and so acquire property and a stake in society. Labouring people have a right to organize themselves into unions, which ideally should be Catholic. Though the Pope thought strikes were sometimes the work of agitators, he thought they were often the result of intolerable conditions. He accepted the right to strike, but thought the state should legislate to remove the grievances that provoke strikes.

Rerum Novarum is one of those historic documents whose importance is hard now to grasp. Leo's attack on unrestricted capitalism, his insistence on the duty of state invervention on behalf of the worker, his assertion of the right to a living wage and the rights of organized labour, changed the terms of all future Catholic discussion of social questions, and gave weight and authority to more adventurous advocates of Social Catholicism. Without being either a democrat or a radical himself, Leo opened the door to the evolution of Catholic democracy.

Rerum Novarum demonstrated that Leo XIII was a more advanced social thinker than most nineteenth-century Catholics.

For many prosperous Irish Catholic businessmen, the Pope Leo XIII Encyclical *Rerum Novarum*, issued in 1891, heralded as great a reformation as Martin Luther's ninety-five theses on indulgences at Wittenberg four centuries before. Did practical businessmen such as the Murphys and indeed their conservative bishops understand *Rerum Novarum*? Could this devout secular audience be expected to accept such a 'fresh insight' into the unchanging papal social teaching?

William Martin Murphy was both radical and devout. His presidential address to the

Cardinal Paul Cullen (1803-78), the architect of Irish Catholicism. Inflexibly opposed to both physical force, nationalism and English influences.
Courtesy St. Patrick's College, Drumcondra

Portrait of Rev. Nicolas Callan, Physicist, 1799-1864 by Leone Glukman c.1850.
Source: *Maynooth College 1791-95 – P. J. Corsh*

Dublin Chamber of Commerce in January 1913 expounded the *Rerum Novarum* message. Obviously he distinguished this from his determination to defeat James Larkin's personal demand for political power through the new weapon of the sympathetic strike. It is worth noting that this 'conspiracy' is still illegal in Ireland and elsewhere. James Plunkett's poignant novel *Strumpet City* (1969) has obscured critical analyses of the William Martin Murphy standpoint. However, the Dublin City Corporation had not the power to improve slum housing and public health until after 1930.

In their newly technical age, the Shipping Murphys must have been involved in the great debate about Darwin's (now somewhat discredited) general theory of evolution. This upset the literal interpretation of the history of creation as described in Genesis. Extremists on both sides greeted this theory as the death of religion. The polymath John Tyndall (1820-93) caused deeply felt upset, particularly amongst the Presbyterian congregation. Rome, however, had learned a little from its disagreement with Galileo.

Perhaps the Murphy brothers might have walked across from The Stephen's Green Club to No. 86 in 1852 to hear John Henry Newman define the roles of religion and science. This was the basis of Newman's *The Idea of a University Defined* (published in 1873). Indeed, the popular Monsignor Gerard Molloy C.M. (1843-1906) and the world-famous Nicholas Callan (1799-1864), Professor of Science at Maynooth College, were widely accepted as explorers in both schools of knowledge.

On the other hand, they had to discuss the unedifying power struggle between the enigmatic Cardinal Paul Cullen (1803-78) and the passionately independent nationalism of that 'Lion of the West' John MacHale (1791-1881), Archbishop of Tuam. The outcome of this lifelong cultural clash would have social consequences for a century or more. Cullen's diplomatically subtle drafting of the Papal Infallibility Decree at the 1870 Vatican Council epitomized their lifelong differences in outlook. The firm of Verdon and Cullen were prosperous livestock exporters in Liverpool even before the Famine. Both the Palgraves and the 'Shipping Murphys' would have come across the Cullens in business.

Literature and the Arts

It is difficult to find any literary celebration of the Irish merchant ships and the merchant navy seamen who sailed them in the century to 1914. Novelists, poets and artists (apart from the historians) saw no inspiration or romance in the rise and fall of these native Irish merchant seamen. This task was left to the journalists, although Arthur Griffith and D. P. Moran did perceive the economic drama.

In the Night Shelter chapter of *Ulysses* James Joyce comments on Griffith's Sinn Féin outlook. The falling off in Irish shipping is regretted. A Palgrave boat was built at Alexandra Basin. However this was the only launch of the year, despite the fact that there were Irish harbours available.

Leopold Bloom had a dream scheme which visualised a tramline linking the Cattle Market with Dublin's Port and Docks where the transit sheds of Palgrave Murphy and Company were situated. The Company were steamship owners, agents for steamers to the Mediterranean and other continental ports.

Some dreams do come true. The proposed Luas Line will extend from Kingsbridge (Heuston) Station to the Point Depot in dockland.

The Pollexfens were merchant ship-owners in the port of Sligo, as the painter Jack B. Yeats recognized. However, his brother, that economical silly-Billy Yeats in the poem *September 1913* could only vent his scorn on the constructive business men such as William Martin Murphy, who –

> …fumble in a greasy till
> And add the halfpence to the pence

William Pollexfen★ (1816-92), the maternal grandfather of W.B. and Jack B. Yeats.
Courtesy: Sligo *by John Cowell*

Casual work on the docks was
one of the few jobs open to
the men of Dublin's tenements.
*Courtesy Daniel Gillman and
Michael O'Connell*

Yeats was a very great lyrical poet but his lofty gaze overlooked the sterling values of John Masefield's *Cargoes*:

> Dirty British coaster with a salt-caked smoke stack
> Butting through the Channel in the mad March days,
> With a cargo of Tyne coal,
> Road-rail, pig-lead,
> Firewood, iron-ware, and cheap tin trays.

There was no Irish Joseph Conrad or Herman Melville to describe our merchant seamen. However, some of their own racy sea shanties have been preserved in Timothy Collins's *The Galway Line*.

The grub was bad, and the wages low,

Leave her, Johnny, leave her!

But now once more ashore we'll go.

This hard teamwork at the capstan continued in the early steamships.

11.2 EXHIBITIONS 1853 TO 1907

The great exhibitions held in nineteenth-century Dublin did mark progressive stages for indigenous businessmen such as the Palgraves and Murphys.

1853 This first big Dublin exhibition marked the end of the Great Irish Famine experience and the slow dawning of the modern economy. It was held on the Royal Dublin Society grounds at Leinster Lawn and was organized, and largely paid for, by William Dargan. Irish industry was given its first showcase.

One-third of the exhibition was devoted to fine art. This developed into the nucleus of the National Gallery of Ireland on the same site provided by the Royal Dublin Society. Dargan's great statue by Thomas Farrell (1827-1900) stands commandingly at the Merrion Square entrance. Queen Victoria visited the exhibition. The thriving alcohol industry became convinced subscribers to arts for the Irish public.

However, George Moore wrote in 1905 suggesting that no one went to the National Gallery except when it rained.

1865 The Dublin International Exhibition opened at the Winter Garden on Earlsfort Terrace and claimed some 700,000 visitors. No doubt Admiral Beechey was there. The Great Hall was subsequently the Aula Maxima of University College Dublin and is now the National Concert Hall.

Charles Dickens visited the exhibition in May 1865 and was surprised at how prosperous Dublin looked, with its magnificent lines of quays along the banks of a bright, unsullied river. The beggars were ever-present. He praised the art collection and the pageantry. The thunderous music of *The Old Hundreth* was most sastisfying. However, the Young Irelanders must have been more critical.

1872 The Dublin Exhibition of Arts, Industries and Manufacturers was also held at Earlsfort Terrace and was designed to promote Irish goods. It was sponsored by the Guinness family. There is no evidence of active support by Palgrave Murphy.

This exhibition was a great success, being open for 154 days, and was visited by 420,000 people.

This enthusiasm inspired the State to take over the Royal Dublin Society Library. The present much-loved National Library of Ireland was opened in 1890.

1900 An Irish Industries Exhibition was held at Windsor, attended by Queen Victoria as her last public function on 18 December 1900. A month later the business world of Dublin would halt to commemorate this symbolic figure of a great trading empire.

1907 January. The (R).I.A.C. Motor Show at the Royal Dublin Society recognised this important commercial potential for modern transport of both persons and goods.

1907 July. King Edward VII and his charming and dignified Consort, Queen Alexandra, visited the Dublin Exhibition in Herbert Park. They were accompanied by the Viceroy and Lady Aberdeen, who were such enthusiastic supporters of Irish

The Exhibition Hall, 1865, on
Earlsfort Terrace, later demolished.
Source: *Illustrated London News*,
(18 March 1865.)
Courtesy J. Brady and A. Simms

Picture Gallery, Upper Central
Hall, Dublin Exhibition, 1865.
Source: *The Dublin Builder* No.101
1 March 1864. Mr. Alfred G. Jones,
Architect

THE MODERN MOSES.

The Exhibition Centre, Herbert Park, 1907, later demolished. (Postcard). *Courtesy: J. Brady and A. Simms*

The Duke of Edinburgh declaring the Dublin Exhibition open at Earlsfort Terrace, June 1872 with the Countess and Earl Spencer, Viceroy.

The Modern Moses Irish International Exhibition 1907.

Irish Automobile Club Show at the Royal Dublin Society, January 1907.

industry. Despite this, the exhibition was fiercely criticized by William Martin Murphy's *Freeman's Journal*, the Gaelic League and others as being primarily devoted to promoting British industry and the Empire. It was deemed by them to be more entertainment and a costly failure – leaving only the Herbert Park site for the unremembering citizens.

Palgrave Murphy subscribed only £250, compared with T. & C. Martin's £500. The City of Dublin Steamship Company contributed £1,000, but the exhibition had little relevance to the shipping industry.

Before modern equipment for reproducing photographs became available, there were numerous commercial artists who worked as illustrators and portraitists. These 'pierhead painters' painted reasonably accurate pictures of ships for the owners and captains. Stormy or calm seas were supplied to order. Such services were available in bigger seaports in Victorian times. Reuben Chappell (1870-1940), the Yorkshire marine artist, provided technically expert paintings of Arklow ships.

Fine examples of these Victorian steamship painters have been preserved by Derek and Geraldine Jones. He is a descendant of Joseph Gough (1849-c.1910) who was master of two Palgrave Murphy steamers as depicted: the *City of Malaga* in 1886 and the *City of Belfast* between 1902 and 1905.

George M. W. Atkinson (c.1806-84) and his artistic family provided some faithful paintings of steamships against their Cork Harbour background. However, W. G. Strickland was dismissive of their marine paintings as 'possessing little merit as pictures'.

The paintings by Admiral R. W. Beechey, R.H.A. (1865-95) did fill in the artistic gap. His 'Royal Mail ship – the *Leinster* – entering Kingstown Harbour' (1868) in a calm sea is a classic which illustrates the current burgeoning economic development.

Daniel Gillman has made a study of the Admiral's career and artistic contribution. The accurately detailed painting of the City of Dublin Steam Packet Company's Royal Mail paddle steamship *Leinster* entering Kingstown Harbour in 1868 is regarded as a historic maritime masterpiece. No doubt the Exhibitions of 1865 and 1872 provided stimulus for the Admiral's labour of love.

Beechey married an Irish lady and retired to live in Ireland in 1864, residing at 2 Belgrave Square, Monkstown, 2 Corrig Castle Terrace, Kingstown, and in Pembroke Road, until returning to England in the late 1870s.

In William A. Coulter's lively scene of the Bull Wall with shipping (dated 1889), there is a steam tug pulling a sailing ship down the Liffey.

Jack B. Yeats' sympathetic drawing *The Pilot* (1912) combines comedy with real life seamen serving the steamer in Sligo harbour.

Irish marine artists of the twentieth century include:

Seán Keating (1889-1977) for Irish Shipping Ltd.

Frank McKelvey (1895-1974) for Kelly's Colliers

Kenneth King is one of the few present-day artists who are consistently dealing with shipping and maritime history.

'Eve' by Patrick MacDowell, R.A.
The Victorian attitude to nudity did not exclude classical statuary.

PRINT COURTESY OF JAMES ADAM & SONS

his last illness. He was President of the Dublin Chamber of Commerce, and for some years was a member of the Dublin Port and Docks Board and of the Irish Lights Board. He was chairman of the Hibernian Bank, of the Dublin, Wicklow, and Wexford Railway Co., and of Bolands Limited, and he was a director of the Dublin Steam Packet Company and of the Cork Steamship Company. His commercial influence will therefore be seen to have been considerable and far-reaching and the many honourable and important positions that he filled sufficiently demonstrate the confidence that his brother commercial men placed in him. Mr. Murphy's magnificent hospitality, when he entertained, as president, the Chambers of Commerce of the Three Kingdoms in the Leinster Hall on the occasion of their visit to Dublin, will not be soon forgotten. His business sagacity, his keen commercial instinct and skill, his prudence and foresight in financial affairs, and the probity and uprightness of his entire character, fitted him admirably for the commercial pursuits in which he was during his life most successful. He was a well known figure in the city, and his death will be regretted by an extensive circle of friends and acquaintances. But his demise will be a cause of sorrow to many besides those to whom he was personally known, for his was a disposition charitable to a bountiful degree, although unostentatious in the extreme. The Catholic charities of the city will especially feel his loss, though consideration of creed could not be said to have influenced him to his beneficence. He was a most generous and liberal subscriber to all the Dublin charities; in fact he denied no appeal of a genuinely charitable kind made to him. He had a host of friends, and was of a most kindly disposition. We do nor think that he ever made any enemy. Unobtrusive and kindly, his genial worth entitled him to many distinctions which his simplicity of character never sought to obtain.

Mr. Murphy leaves three sons and a daughter; Mrs. Murphy, his beloved wife, died some four years ago. The funeral will leave 21 Merrion Square tomorrow morning, at 9.30 a.m., for Dean's Grange Cemetery.

12.1 d. JOHN MURPHY (1841-1924) AND HIS DESCENDANTS

John Murphy, the eldest son of Michael Murphy II, J.P., was baptized on 24 October 1841 at St. Andrew's, Westland Row. He was a partner in the family's shipping firm, Palgrave Murphy & Company, where he was apparently in charge of office administration. It is important to note that the Statutory Shipping Registers show John

Murphy as the beneficial owner/manager of the ships. It is he who was legally recognized as the 'ship's husband', responsible for its entering and leaving, as well as the day-to-day provisions and repairs while in port. Seamen traditionally thought of their ships as feminine creatures, having womanly qualities and needs – part mother, part harpy. Political correctness was unheard of.

John Murphy resided in Avondale, 11 Avoca Avenue from about 1877 until his death in 1924. In 1862 he joined his contemporaries of T. & C. Martin★ as members of The Stephen's Green Club. He held £3,000 nominal stock value £4,590 in City of Dublin Steam Packet Co. Ltd. and served as a director of the company until it was finally wound up in 1924, having been amalgamated with the B & I Co. (Coast Lines) in 1919. He was consul for Belgium.

His wife Anne, née Byrne, had predeceased him. They had four sons and two daughters. John Murphy died on 26 October 1924 aged eighty-three, leaving an impressive gross personal wealth of £156,040 (before Death Duty £29,435) and was buried in Dean's Grange Cemetery, like his father.

His will, dated 22 April 1922, listed his family:

Joseph Xavier	– Son – Successor and Co-Executor
Francis D'Assissi	– Son
Michael Joseph	– Son – in Trust
John Joseph	– Son – in Trust
Mrs. Mary Anne Browne	– Daughter
She eventually sold	
Avondale to J.H. Pigot	
in 1925	
Captain Ian Grant	– Husband of Anne – £3,000

and various nieces and nephews,
as well as bequests to his household servants:

Catherine Green, Housekeeper	£ 1,000
Anna Whelan	£ 250
Peter Fee, Coachman	£ 50
Thomas Campbell, Gardner	£ 50
Paul Heslip, Chauffeur (for the 1910 Panhard)	£ 50
and other servants	@ £30/£40

Avondale (No.11) and *Altadore* (No.13) were dignified, spacious residences on Avoca Avenue in the recently formed and active township of Blackrock.

The villa-style houses on Avoca Avenue were eminently suitable for these newly successful businessmen in their forties. The development was on a part of the Proby Deer Park. The lease was for 200 years from 1876 @ £21 p.a. There were four reception rooms and four or five bedrooms, with two servants' rooms. Avondale (Poor Law Valuation £60), where John Murphy lived from *c*.1862 until his death in 1924, stood on a secluded site of approximately one acre. It was then sold to Judge Pigot.

Avoca Avenue, where these Murphys lived, was in the Roman Catholic parish of Booterstown, which then included Blackrock. The new Blackrock church,★ designed by his brother-in-law Patrick J. Byrne in the Pugin style, was completed between 1845 and 1850. No doubt the Murphy family assisted in the collections to finance the necessary explosion of churches and schools which catered for this expanding development area surrounding them. Canon Forde, who was Parish Priest from 1862 to 1873, overhauled Booterstown church and parochial house. The Parish Priest at the time of the divisive 1913 strike was Monsignor O'Donnell, who was Parish Priest of Booterstown from 1904 to 1922.

TOP LEFT:
Avondale, No. 11 Avoca Avenue was the residence of John Murphy from c.1862 until his death in 1924. *Courtesy Irish Architectural Archive*

'An outstanding Victorian residence on over an acre. A prestige home of quality and character'. Auction Notice 1938.

TOP:
Altadore, Avoca Avenue was the residence of (Sir) James Murphy prior to his move to 'Yapton' in Monkstown. *Courtesy Irish Architectural Archive*

Presumably because the construction of that church did not lend itself to large stained-glass windows,★ it was to St. John the Baptist, Blackrock that the Murphy family presented the Harry Clarke windows in 1925.

(Sir) James Murphy's *Altadore* (PLV £44) was somewhat smaller, on a half-acre site. His father Michael Murphy II, J.P. appeared as the owner in 1859. James lived there from 1877 until c.1912 when he moved to his much more upmarket residence at *Yapton*, Monkstown. He was succeeded by his son James, who lived there until 1906. This house is not to be confused with Altadore (now a Nursing Home) in Glenageary.

The *Dublin Builder* of 1 July 1860 (courtesy the Irish Architectural Archive) recorded that three villas and offices are to be built at Avoca Avenue, Blackrock – Mr. Edward H. Carson, Architect. Again on 1 May 1864 a very modest villa built for E. Alma Esquire, Builder Gregory Murphy of Williamstown, cost £1,000, Architect Edward H. Carson. Presumably *Avondale* and *Altadore* were designed by him for the developer and sold by auction to the Murphys.

Edward Henry Carson (1832-81) was the father of Lord Edward Carson, the anti Home Rule leader whose unconstitutional activities caused the weak Liberal Prime Minister Herbert Asquith great grief. E. L. Alma was a solicitor and property developer, who gave his name to the 'sea fields' in Blackrock. He provided local information to surveyor John O'Donovan for the Royal Commission of 1836.

The *Dublin Builder* described the development in 1862 as:

Amongst the numerous and most recent architectural acquisitions in the shape of domestic structures in the neighbourhood of Blackrock, Co. Dublin, are especially noticeable dwelling houses just finished in Avoca Avenue, a few minutes walk from the town and railway station, and central in a most delightful and beautiful locality, where many of the elite of the metropolis have their suburban residences. Of somewhat Italian and Byzantine style of architecture combined, the exterior of these houses is remarkably effective, and, what is better, displays taste and judgement in the ornamental accessories, a compliment we are not always permitted the pleasure of paying the architects of similar class of structures generally in the vicinity of Dublin, who often sacrifice those very desirable ingredients to profuseness of ornament which may please the vulgar eye but is by no means artistically orthodox.

Comprehensive culinary offices, pantries, servants'-room, water closet, etc. are unexceptionable, and we doubt not will be found ample to meet every probable requirement.

Modern conveniences, such as damp course drainage, water closet and bath with hot and cold water, are not described. No doubt the Michael Murphy (Junior) Company would provide coal for heating and the cooking range. The Kingstown Gas Company (1864) did not extend to Avoca Avenue at that time. The supply of electricity came a generation later.

Obituary Notice – *The Irish Times*, 27 October 1926

MR. JOHN MURPHY

We regret to announce the death, on Saturday last, of Mr. John Murphy at his residence Avondale, Blackrock. Mr. Murphy, who was in his eighty-fourth year, was a highly respected citizen of Dublin and a very successful man in business. He was a member of the ship-owning firm of Palgrave Murphy & Company and one of a family who have attained distinction in the commercial community.

Mr. Murphy was a brother of Sir Michael Murphy and of the late Sir James Murphy. He, like his brothers, was offered a title several years ago but he declined it. He was for many years Chairman of the Hibernian Bank a position which, to the regret of his colleagues, he resigned a couple of years ago finding that, owing to advancing years, the place should be filled by a younger man. For a considerable period of the tenure of the Hibernian Bank Mr. Murphy was also Chairman of the Alliance & Dublin Gas Company. Unable to continue, his colleagues acquiesced to his withdrawal. He was remarkably active for a man of his years. His statements to the shareholders of the Gas Company were models of fairness and directness. Mr. Murphy was a gentleman of genial temperament and was very popular with the officials of the companies with which he had been associated. His son, Mr. Joseph Xavier Murphy, succeeded him as director of the Gas Company.

JOSEPH XAVIER MURPHY (1860-1937) of Ashurst, Mount Merrion Avenue, was a son and the successor of John Murphy. Joseph Xavier worked at Palgrave Murphy all his life until the disposal. His estate was valued for probate at £68,000 gross. His widow was Norah, née Fottrell.

Issue

His son   – Owen Joseph Murphy (father of Primrose Murphy), stockbroker, was his co-executor.

daughter   – Sheelah Murphy, married firstly Henry FitzHerbert and secondly Owen Martin, who died in 1945.

son   – Ronald, regular soldier in the British Army, who died in 1942.

As well as succeeding his father in charge of Palgrave Murphy, Joseph Xavier was a director of the Alliance & Dublin Gas Company, Great Southern Railways, Bank of Ireland (of which he became Governor) and other companies.

Joseph Xavier conducted the protracted negotiations with Lloyd's Insurance and with the British and German governments for reparations concerning the Palgrave Murphy ships, cargoes and crews lost during World War I. The settlement was reduced because of the insolvency of the German Republic. This management decision to sell off most of the remaining Palgrave Murphy ships during the short-lived post-war boom was justified. Two years of phenomenal activity were followed by a prolonged shipping slump. The spectacular rise and collapse of Amalgamated Industrials Ltd.★ in 1920-22 had consequential repercussions in Dublin.

Joseph Xavier Murphy represented the South Dublin constituency as an independent member of the Dáil from 1927 to 1932, but did not seek re-election thereafter.

FRANCIS (FRANK), D'ASSISSI MURPHY (*c.*1879-1900), son of John Murphy (1841-1924) and his wife Anne, née Byrne. Frank married Marguerite Casella in 1909. They had seven sons and two daughters.

After Dublin University he joined the Royal Field Artillery. He worked for Palgrave Murphy & Company at Bristol before the Great War. After 1918 Frank retired to Devon where his only surviving son, Major M. D. Murphy, now lives.

In 1924 his father, John, bequeathed:

(a) £25,000; (b) 'and also the policy of insurance effected on my life with The London Insurance Corporation'; (c) and a one-quarter share in the claim for loss and internment of ships in Germany; (d) and half of the residue.

OWEN JOSEPH MURPHY (c.1904-44), Stockbroker – 50% partner M. Dillon & Son – of Druid Hill, Killiney and formerly of Rostrevor Road, Rathgar, was the elder son of Joseph Xavier and a grandson of John Murphy.

He died on 30 December 1944, aged thirty-nine, at 33 Upper Fitwilliam Street, leaving a wife, Rosemary, as his Executrix, and four children, Dinah, Roderick, Linda and Primrose.

12.1 E. SIR JAMES JOSEPH MURPHY, BART, JP, DL (1843-1922)

Sir James Joseph Murphy of *Yapton*, Monkstown and formerly of *Altadore*, Avoca Avenue, Blackrock, was created a Knight in 1902 and a Baronet of the United Kingdom in 1903. He was also made a Deputy Lieutenant for the city of Dublin. This social status is dealt with in Chapter 9. Sir James was the second son of Michael Murphy II, J.P. He was the most prominent public figure of the Palgrave Murphy executives, although his youngest brother, Sir Michael III, was more entrepreneurial.

Sir James Murphy, 1843-1922

He married Brigid Jane Norman in 1869 and had a son, James Mark II, born in 1879, who sadly died in 1921, and five daughters.

Sir James was a very important person in his native city. He was a director of the Palgrave Murphy & Company partnership, Michael Murphy Ltd., Cork Steamship Company Ltd., Dublin Port & Docks Board, and Dublin Chamber of Commerce, which he joined in 1865, becoming President in 1902-04. He was chairman of the Royal Bank.

He was involved in the power struggle against the nationalist Dublin Corporation. As a Liberal Unionist, he supported the Royal Family. Whatever were his views (or those of his daughter Katherine, who was a nun) about *Rerum Novarum*, his shipping interests were in the forefront in the defeat of Larkin's 1913 strike.

Club memberships were socially important for the Victorians. Sir James's clubs were The Stephen's Green, Constitutional, London and the Royal Irish Yacht (he had been an excellent yachtsman). The July 1914 gun-running activities of fellow yachtsmen such as Sir Thomas Myles, Conor O'Brien and Erskine Childers was succeeded by their active service for the allies against Germany. There was indeed room for that heated debate which is ongoing. Incidentally The Stephen's Green Club and the Royal Irish were twin foundations of the O'Connells and their Catholic and Quaker Liberal associates.

Since the Palgrave Murphy ships served the ports of Dortmund and Hamburg, it was important for Sir James to be Consul for the Imperial German Empire. He took over his father's connection. The Great War★ shattered the love/hate relationship between the British Royal Family and their German cousin Kaiser Wilhelm II (1859-1941). No doubt Sir James was involved socially in that tendentious visit of the German fleet under the command of Prince Henry of Prussia to Kingstown Harbour just three years before the outbreak of war. He also concerned himself in the coronation visit of King George V in 1911.

As Consul, Sir James must have been disturbed by reports in the *Freeman's Journal* that friends of the Kaiser were involved in a homosexual scandal. In the strict privacy of The Stephen's Green Club, the similar lifestyle of an important clique in the Castle was discussed in scandalized secrecy. In 1907 that hushed-up enquiry into the theft of the 'Irish Crown Jewels' added smoke to the flame. Investigative journalists were still curbed by the establishments at Dublin Castle and Maynooth College. Only seven years previously the ostracized Oscar Wilde from Merrion Square had suffered his lonely impoverished death at the Hotel d'Alsace in Paris. His poignant *Ballad of Reading Gaol* remained fresh in Dublin's memories.

Sir James must have known about the successful Hibernian Coal and Steel Syndicates in the Ruhr organized by William Thomas Mulvany (1806-85). Palgrave Murphy carried competitive German manufactured goods from Hamburg to British and Irish ports.

The huge financial reparations imposed by Germany after the Franco-Prussian War of 1870-71 enabled German manufacturers to modernize so as to compete successfully with the mature British importers.

Yapton on Carrickbrennan Road in Monkstown was Sir James's suitably impressive residence from 1906 until his death on 16 June 1922. Then it was apparently vacant for some years when Mrs. M. Bagot took over until the Sacred Heart School opened in 1945. This Regency-style house was built by Thomas Hone, the property developer, about 1840.

Thomas Martin of T. & C. Martin, the timber importers and shipowners, who was the father of Mother Mary Martin, lived in the adjoining house, 'Greenbank', from about 1890. His widow continued to live there. In April 1947 the house and grounds were handed over by Mother Mary Martin personally to the Sacred Heart School. The school closed in 1977 because of the financial difficulties and a shortage of vocations. Both houses were demolished for residential development.

The Irish Times of 17 February 1922 noted the death of a great shipowner Sir James Murphy.

Failing health had for some time compelled him to withdraw from his active business duties but a hope was entertained until quite recently that he might yet be spared to resume the prominent position he held in the commercial life of Dublin. The hope has, to the sincere regret of his many friends, been disappointed.

Sir James Murphy was the second son of Mr. Michael Murphy, J.P., of Merrion Square, Dublin. He was born in January 1843 and early in life he became connected with the shipping industry, in which he had a most successful career, culminating in his becoming head of the firm of Messrs. Palgrave, Murphy & Co., Eden Quay, a prosperous company of steamship owners, trading chiefly to Mediterranean ports.

Sir James Murphy was a keen man of business. Although the affairs of his own company claimed his close personal attention, he took an active interest in all movements which concerned the welfare of Dublin Port and of the city. He occupied for several years a seat at the Port and Docks Board, and he held the office of chairman. His advice on various questions affecting the welfare of the port was always received with the respect due to his position and experience in the shipping industry – an industry whose revival in Dublin he did much to promote.

Sir James was also a valued member of the Dublin Chamber of Commerce, and on three separate occasions he had been its president. In the Chamber he revealed a wide knowledge of various branches of business, and his support was always available on behalf of any proposal to promote and develop local industries. He was also closely associated with the banking interest in Dublin, and for several years he filled the post of chairman of the Royal Bank.

He was a Justice of the Peace and a Deputy Lieutenant for the City of Dublin. In recognition of his public services he received the honour of knighthood in 1902, and was created a baronet in the following year.

He married in 1869 Bridget Jane, daughter of Francis Norman, a prominent Dublin solicitor, by whom he had five daughters (one of whom is a nun) and one son, who died last year.

Sir James Murphy was a man of kindly nature, and was held in the highest respect by his numerous employees. He was a devout member of the Roman Catholic Church, and a large contributor to its various charities. His loss will be keenly felt in the commercial life of Dublin. He was a member of the Constitutional and the Royal

Irish Yacht Clubs, and in early life was an excellent yachtsman.

Before the war Sir James was German Consul in Dublin.

The Port and Docks Board flag, the Palgrave Murphy Company's flag, and the flags of other companies were flown at half-mast yesterday when the news of Sir James Murphy's death became known along the Liffey.

12.1 F. SIR MICHAEL MURPHY ('JUNIOR') III (1847-1925) and his descendants. Sir Michael Murphy ('Junior') III, BART. of the United Kingdom created 1912, of 'Wyckham', Dundrum and 88 Merrion Square, Dublin (now occupied by the National Gallery of Ireland) and formerly of *Altadore*, Avoca Avenue, Blackrock.

(Sir) Michael married Mary Freeman in 1877 and had 2 sons, Arthur c.1880, predeceased; (Sir) George born c.1881, died c.1930, and 3 daughters, Frances and Jane predeceased, and Beatrice, Lady O'Loghlen, born c.1879.

(Sir) Michael III struck out on his own from Palgrave Murphy & Company. He became a self-made coal merchant who thrived on the expanding coal business in Dublin. There was strong competition from the mainly Protestant establishment, not only of Dublin, but also from Belfast and Liverpool. The profits of this separate trade were not included in the Palgrave Murphy partnership accounts.

Hazel P. Smyth records this saga:

> Until steam tugs took over, coal was imported in small sailing colliers. The trade was revolutionized by big steam ships. the firm of Michael Murphy was founded in the 1870s by Michael Murphy III – later Sir Michael, the third son of the head of Palgrave Murphy & Company. Both the father and the son were partners in Palgrave Murphy & Company. To avoid confusion in the names, the trade name of Michael Murphy Junior was used for some years. Its offices were at 37 Eden Quay where it carried on a successful business carrying coal from the Bristol Channel to Dublin and Cork for the Irish railways.
>
> A few years after the formation of this Murphy company another company was set up under the title of Dublin & General Steam Shipping Company, Michael Murphy being the proprietor of both companies. In 1889 Michael Murphy III entered the general cargo business and inaugurated services between Dublin, Cardiff and Liverpool. The business was wound up in 1932 and the B & I took over. Five ships were built in Dublin between 1908 and 1921.

To·all·and·singular·as·well—
...lemen as Gentlemen and others to whom these Presents shall come, I, Captai...
...eville Rodwell Wilkinson C·V·O, J·P, A·R·E, Ulster King of Arm...
...Principal Herald of All Ireland, Registrar of the Most Illustrious Order of...
...nt Patrick, send due Salutations and Greeting, Whereas applicati...
...h been made unto me by Sir Michael Murphy of Wyckham in t...
...unty of Dublin and 88 Merrion Square in the City of Dublin, Baronet...
...ting forth that he is desirous that Armorial Ensigns may be truly marshall...
... assigned by lawful authority unto him and his descendants such as wil...
...injury or prejudice to any other he and they may forever hereafter bear a...
...ance and that the same may be registered and recorded in the Office...
...ster King of Arms in Ireland, to the end that the Officers of Arms the...
... all others upon occasion may take full notice and have knowledge there...
... he hath therefore prayed that I would grant and assign unto him an...
...descendants such Armorial Ensigns as he and they may lawfully use a...
... Know Ye therefore that I the said Ulster King of Arms hav...
...en the request of the said applicant into consideration and having exam...

It is mere fantasy to imagine that (Sir) Michael Murphy III might have imported coal from the colliery of his contemporary Edward Smith (1805-80).★

The 1901 Census recorded (Sir) Michael at 88 Merrion Square West as being a widower, steamship owner, Catholic, born in County Dublin. His household consisted of:

Beatrice	22	daughter, single	(married O'Loghlen)
Arthur	21	son, steamship owner, single	(died January 1919)
George	19	son, steamship owner, single	(who succeeded Sir Michael)
Emily		Governess and three servants	

He celebrated his title in 1912 by engaging Sir Neville R. Wilkinson K.C.V.O., J.P., Ulster King of Arms and Principal Herald of all Ireland, to prepare his armorial★ ensigns by His Majesty's Letters Patent under the Great Seal of Ireland. These arms and crest were impressive at that time.

'Is maith an maiseach le sean brog bucla'
(a buckle makes a good ornament for an old shoe)

'Wyckham', Dundrum, was the residence of Sir Michael Murphy. In 1925 Simpson's Hospital acquired the house as a home for the elderly.
Courtesy Peter Pearson

Armorial Ensigns obtained by Sir Michael Murphy in 1912.

-121-

'Wyckham' on the Ballinteer Road has been fully described by Peter Pearson. It is a large late-Georgian house of about 1800, which was enlarged during the nineteenth century. Sir Michael III moved there c.1912. The Murphy Estate sold 'Wyckham' to Simpson's Hospital for the elderly in 1925. The name survives as the Wyckham By-Pass.

(Sir) Michael Murphy III used his considerable influence to have ship-building and repairs resumed in Dublin. In 1885 the Port and Docks Graving Dock was used by him for repairing his ships. Between 1908 and 1921 five of his steamers were built in Dublin: *Enda*, *Finola*, *Patricia (II)*, *Rhona*, and *Rosaleen* (ex *Ita*).

James Joyce★ recognized the topical importance of Irish shipping.

(Sir) Michael Murphy III served on the Dublin Port and Docks Board from 1868 to 1914, being Chairman in 1903, and on the Chamber of Commerce from 1890 to 1914, being President in 1891-93. He was also a director of the Belfast Bank.

His clubs were The Stephen's Green, Dublin, and Reform, London. Both clubs were of liberal outlook. He may have been a member of the Royal Irish Yacht Club, like his brother Sir James.

At the turn of the nineteenth century there were stormy political seas to be chartered by this practical steamship owner. His business could cope with the Home Ruler's version of Sinn Féin. How could he survive the revolutionary ideas of Connolly, Larkin and the Fenianism of the Irish Republican Brotherhood's army?

When (Sir) Michael died at 'Wyckham' on 30 June 1925, he was buried like his father in Dean's Grange Cemetery. His world had changed utterly. However, the assets were valued for 19% Estate Duty at £211,210. This included his share of the troublesome settlement of reparation claims against his former associates in the German government for seizure of ships during World War I.

ARTHUR DANIEL MURPHY was born in 1880. He was a son of Sir Michael Murphy III, whom he predeceased.

The 1901 Census recorded Arthur as residing at 88 Merrion Square with his father, his brother (Sir) George and sister Beatrice. Arthur was described as a shipowner, aged twenty-one and single. He was a director of Michael Murphy Ltd., holding some shares; and M. J. Begg Ltd., holding five shares.

The steamer *Arthur* was named after him in 1894.

Arthur died unmarried on 25 January 1919 at his father's residence 'Wyckham', Dundrum.

(SIR) GEORGE BERNARD MURPHY (1881-1963), second Baronet, was the only surviving son of Sir Michael Murphy III, then of 88 Merrion Square. His brother Arthur (1880-1919) had predeceased him.

The steamer *George* was named after him in 1894.

Sir George died at his residence, 'Hawthorn', 24 Shrewsbury Road in the Pembroke Borough on 4 July 1963. His Estate was valued at £371,678, attracting Irish Estate Duty @ 40%. Sir Michael III left his property equally between Sir George and his sister Beatrice (O'Loghlen). The shares in Michael Murphy Limited went to Sir George.

Michael Murphy Limited was taken over by B & I (Coast Lines) in 1926. However the agency company, M. J. Begg & Co. Ltd. of Cardiff and No. 3 Beresford Place, continued to function. Sir George served as a director until liquidation in 1936 and had held 2,971 shares @ £10 each.

He became a director of the National Bank in 1926 and was on the Board of the Alliance & Dublin Gas Company. He was briefly on the Dublin Port and Docks Board and the Chamber of Commerce *c.*1921/22.

In 1913 he married Frances, daughter of the well-known solicitor Richard Davoren, who lived at 'Friarsland', Roebuck in Dundrum. They were childless. She survived Sir George and was an Executor. The Will provided for the widow and her two sisters, Esmay O'Farell and Carman Davoren. There was a trust for charities of £10,000 divided in equal shares among: St. Vincent De Paul; Little Sisters of the Poor; Royal Alfred Aged Merchant Seamen's Institute, 58 Fenchurch Street, London; Royal U.K. Beneficent Association; and Royal Hospital for Incurables, Donnybrook.

BEATRICE O'LOGHLEN was born in 1879, being the daughter of Sir Michael Murphy III. On her father's death in 1925, she inherited one-half of his property (excluding the shares in Michael Murphy Limited) and was co-executor with her brother (Sir) George Murphy.

The steamship *Beatrice* was named after her in 1889.

She married (Sir) Michael O'Loghlen, Barrister, afterwards Judge, of Ennis, Co. Clare.

12.2 PALGRAVE FAMILY TREE

PALGRAVE	BORN	DIED	RESIDED	OCCUPATION
Thomas	1715	1775	Yarmouth	Master of Privateer East India Co.
William I	1745	1822	Yarmouth	Owned land & malt houses Mayor 1782 and 1805
William II	1771	1847	Yarmouth To Dublin c.1825	Owned malt houses etc. Also Collector of customs dues. Married Elizabeth Barker 10 children, including William III – and Charles George 1818-93 of Palgrave Murphy
William Barker III	1802	1857		Dublin Shipping Agency with Charles. Did not marry.

CHILDREN OF WILLIAM PALGRAVE II Married Elizabeth née Barker c.1798

BORN	DIED	SONS	
c.1800	1801	William	– died young
1802	1857	William Barker III	– shipping, Dublin
1804	c.1895	Thomas	– lawyer, Wales
1812	1841	Robert	– medicine, Trinity College, Dublin
1814	1868	John	– Custom House, Dublin and London
1818	1893	Charles George	– of Palgrave Murphy & Company

BORN	DAUGHTERS	MARRIED
c.1801	Elizabeth Matilda	– John Kerr, Bristol
1805	Mary Elizabeth	– Henry Woodhouse
1816	Katherine	– James Wood of Liverpool
1820	Jane Ann	– Quintan Fleming of Dublin and Liverpool

Apparently all the children were born in Great Yarmouth before the move to Dublin c.1825.

The Perlustration of Great Yarmouth by CHARLES PALMER, 1872

The Palgrave lineage is fully described in the inimitable *The Perlustration*. Local research has been skilfully provided by Gill McKenna.

When the older branch of the Palgraves of Pulham, who claimed to be the next heirs male, became extinct in the male line, the representation of this ancient family is believed to have devolved on the Palgraves of Yarmouth, who traced their descent from the Rev. Robert Palgrave of Bealings in Suffolk, who, it is asserted, was the third son of William Palgrave, fourth son of Thomas Palgrave by Christian his wife, daughter of John Sayer of Pulman, and which said Thomas Palgrave was the son of Thomas Palgrave of Pulham, who died in 1545, son of Robert Palgrave of Gunton, Norfolk, second son of John de Palgrave of Norwood Berningham by Sybilla de Hetherset his wife. The Rev. Robert Palgrave settled in Yarmouth, where he died in 1737, aged 81. Robert Palgrave, his son, married Hannah Bacon, and died in 1741, leaving a son, Thomas Palgrave, who married Mary Manning of Southtown. He entered the service of the East India Company, and commanded one of their ships. He was one of the elder brethren of the corporation of the Trinity House; and retiring to Yarmouth purchased an estate at Coltishall in Norfolk, where he died in 1775, aged 62 years. William Palgrave, his elder son, married Elizabeth, daughter of Robert Thirkettle of Flegg Burgh, Norfolk. He filled the office of mayor in 1782, and again in 1805, and took a leading part in politics; strenuously supporting the principles of Mr. Coke of Holkham, and the pretensions of the Anson family to the representation of the borough in Parliament. Having retired to his estate at Coltishall, he died there in 1822, aged 77.

William Palgrave II, his eldest son★, filled the office of mayor in 1814. The inquest which elected him 'laid from Monday noon until Wednesday afternoon' before they could agree....

The library, formerly the Custom House, was leased in 1775 to James Turner, Esq., who, when admitted a partner in the firm of Gurneys and Co., of Norwich, closed the tavern and converted the premises to the purposes of a bank. The banking business having been removed to the Hall Plain, the old house was purchased in 1807 by Samuel Barker, Esq., who removed the Three Cranes, and erected on the site a spacious mansion for the residence of William Palgrave, jun., Esq., who had married his daughter.

It is said that the sum of £1,000 was paid for the site. The bricks with which the

William Palgrave I (1745-1822) Mayor of Great Yarmouth, Merchant and Farmer at Coltis Hall.

South Quay, Great Yarmouth, playground of Gifford Palgrave and his brothers when they visited 'Grandpapa at the Bank'– the tall building fourth from the left.
Courtesy Palgrave of Arabia *by Mea Allan*

new house was erected were manufactured on the Holkham estate, and were presented by T. W. Coke, Esq.,★ (afterwards Earl of Leicester), with whom the Palgraves, father and son, were long on terms of political and social intercourse. In a series of letters addressed by the Rev. Wenman Langton, Rector of Warham in Norfolk from 1789 to 1837, to Mr. Palgrave, and now in the possession of his grandson, Thomas Palgrave, Esq., frequent allusion is made to visits paid by Mr. Palgrave to Mr. Coke at Holkham, especially during the time of the annual sheep shearing, when that eminent agriculturist was, for many years, accustomed to receive numerous illustrious and distinguished guests, including the late Dukes of Gloucester and Sussex, and that great scholar, Dr. Parr.

William Palgrave II★ removed to Dublin on being promoted to the collectorship in that city, and died there in 1839, aged 69 years.

His two surviving sons, Thomas Palgrave, Esq., J. P. of Llansantffraid near Conway, North Wales, and Charles Palgrave, Esq., of Dublin, claim to be heirs male to the Palgraves of Norwood Berningham.

William Palgrave, the elder, had two other sons who attained manhood, namely, Robert Palgrave who, after distinguishing himself at Cambridge, accepted the office

As if that soul were fled: /over
So sleeps the pride of former days,
So glory's thrill is o'er,
And hearts that once beat high for praise,
Now feel its pulse no more!

Just such a traditional ballad would still cause political angst at the Misses Morkan's annual dance (*The Dead*, James Joyce).

THOMAS LEVINS MOORE of Dundalk was a brewer who was prominent in racing and hunting. He and his partner, Sir Thomas C. Macardle, were members of The Stephen's Green Club.

John Murphy by will dated 22 April 1922 appointed 'my friend Thomas Levins Moore' as an executor with a legacy of £100. In the event, he did not join in the application for the grant of probate in 1924.

Michael Bernard Mullins
Courtesy Institution of Engineers of Ireland

MICHAEL BERNARD MULLINS, J.P. C.E. (1800-71) was the architect who undertook the renovation of 9 St. Stephen's Green for The Stephen's Green Club during 1840-45. There he would have socialized with the 'Shipping Murphys'. However, most of his work was in construction and drainage works.

The *Irish Builder* noted that he left £30,000 to endow the 'Mullins Convalescent Home' on land donated by Francis Coppinger of Monkstown Castle. Mullins's legacy was put to good use in the building of the 'Linden Convalescent Home for the poor in Stillorgan', founded by the Irish Sisters of Charity.★ Sadly, these elegant buildings have mostly been demolished.

WILLIAM MURPHY (*c.*1830–*c.*1893) was a coal importer and ship owner at 9 Lower Sackville Street. There was an office at College Green in the 1890s. He lived at number 20 in the newly built Kenilworth Square and at 10 Mountjoy Square. This William Murphy's relationship, if any, to the 'Shipping Murphys' has not been identified. However, the business connection was important in the early development stage of the Palgrave Murphy company. Be that as it may, researches of the Registers have failed to uncover his family history.

William Martin Murphy.
Organiser of the Exhibition,
owner of the Dublin Tram
company, Clerys and the Irish
Independent group, as well as
extensive overseas interests.
Courtesy Peter Costello

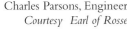

Charles Parsons, Engineer
Courtesy Earl of Rosse

Apparently he was the son of William H. Murphy, master mariner, coal factor and proprietor of the Manx Arms Hotel at 37 Fleet Street, and followed in his father's business.

In 1895 a William Murphy was the owner of the sailing ship St. Joseph, registered in Dublin but built in America in 1865. Two years later the sailing ship Westminister,★ built in Quebec, was registered in the name of W. Murphy.

WILLIAM MARTIN MURPHY (1844-1919) was a powerful entrepreneur in railways, tramways and *The Irish Independent* and *Freeman's Journal* newspapers. Arguably he was the most successful Irish entrepreneur ever. As such, however, he was scorned by the poet W. B. Yeats. He was prominent in the Employers Federation during the Larkin strikes★ of 1913. At the same time, however, he was a radical Home Ruler and a member of Parliament, who refused to accept a title.

William Martin Murphy was not a relation of his contemporaries the 'Shipping Murphys'. He served with them on the Dublin Chamber of Commerce and the Dublin Port and Docks Board.

EDGAR JAMES PAINE, Solicitor, was appointed Co-Executor of Charles G. Palgrave by will dated 8 January 1887, drawn up by Paine & Company.

He was a partner in the firm of Paine & Company of 14 St. Helen's Place, London. He lived at Bedford House, Seaford, Sussex.

It was Sir Thomas Paine who conducted the successful negotiations with Hollams, Solicitors of Mincing Lane, for the agreement with Michael Murphy II on the dissolution of the Palgrave Murphy & Company partnership.

CHARLES PARSONS, FRS., KCB. (1851-1931) was a son of the astronomer Earl of Rosse of Birr Castle.

He distinguished himself in mathematics in Trinity College Dublin and in Cambridge University. By 1894 his work on steam turbines was successful. Three years later his famous 'Turbinia' demonstrated that the triple expansion steam engine was out of date for merchant navy shipping fleets. Parsons also controlled the firm of Sir Howard Grubb & Sons, makers of optical and astonomical instuments.

EBENEZER PIKE and his sons Joseph and Ebenezer were chairmen of the Cork Steamship Company Ltd. This prosperous company operated from 1843 until it was taken over by the ill-fated Amalgamated Industrials Ltd.★ in 1920-22.

In the eighteenth century Joseph Pike and his family were prominent Quakers (Appendix 14.6). Their prosperous wool-exporting business in Clonmel expanded into merchant banking facilities.

'The Cork Card Case' was a *cause célèbre* in which the privacy of Cork's Unionist Club was exposed for the enjoyment of the public. Joseph Pike D.L. was accused of cheating at cards. Following the unfortunate precedent of the Tranby Croft scandal involving Prince Edward, an attempt was made to hush up the incident. However, R.P. Beamish D.L., as Trustee, decided that the allegation should be investigated. Pike took a libel action. On 23 May 1894, the Dublin jury found in his favour.

EDWARD SMITH (1805-80) emigrated from Annalong, County Down in 1821. King Coal raised him from rags to riches in that laissez-faire dockland of pre-Famine Liverpool. He was a contemporary of William Palgrave II and Michael Murphy II, J.P.

Edward Smith owned the Chapel House Collieries, Liverpool, and Bellamont Forest in County Cavan. He owned three schooners which carried the Chapel House coal across to the yard which he had established at Rostrevor Harbour in his native County Down. John Prenderville, the Mersey steam tug owner, was his life-long friend.

In 1867 Edward Smith married, secondly, Isabella Cullen (1846-1923). Her father, James Cullen (1800-91), a railway engineer with George Stephenson, was a first cousin of Cardinal Paul Cullen,★ whose brothers were partners in Verdon & Cullen, cattle importers, Liverpool.

Edward's daughter Isabella Anne (1879-1945) married in London Dr. Frederick P. Smith, D.L. (1864-1943) of Kevit Castle, County Cavan. They represented their country at the coronation of King George V in Westminster Abbey in May 1910.

The author is one of their eight children.

BINDON BLOOD STONEY, L.L.D. (HONS) F.R.S. was chief engineer of the Dublin Port & Docks Board from 1862 to 1898. Six years earlier he had been appointed assistant to George Halpin Junior (of lighthouse fame) who had succeeded his father in the post of engineer in 1854. Halpin resigned in 1864. He does not appear to be related to Captain Robert Charles Halpin.★ Dr. Stoney was a brilliant engineer and a forceful administrator in the development of the Port for half a century.

Dr. Stoney was a contemporary of Michael Murphy II, J.P.

THOMAS WEBB (1806-84), Quaker businessman, Nationalist and anti-slavery campaigner, joined Bewley to establish their dockyard in 1862.

JOHN R. WIGHAM (1829-1906) of Albany House, Monkstown, was one of the numerous Quaker★ contemporaries who contributed to Irish maritime history. He was Chairman of Joshua Edmundson's Engineering Company in Capel Street where Leslie Green strove to continue those traditions into modern times.

He battled to secure publication of his newly invented and impressively better kind of lamp in lighthouses. Previously oil lights were in use. He also wired steamships for electricity.

John Wigham served on the Quaker committee for the preservation of life at sea and was, like Jonathan Hogg and the Pims, a supporter of Gladstone's Home Rule Bill.

Bindon Blood Stoney, chief engineer to the Port Board from 1862 to 1898.
Courtesy: Dublin Port and Docks Board

George Halpin Junior, chief engineer to the port board, 1854-62.
Courtesy Port of Dublin *by H.A. Gilligan*

12.4 B. THE CONTEMPORARIES OF THE PALGRAVE FAMILY

THOMAS WILLIAM COKE (1752–1842) of Holkham in Norfolk, afterwards Earl of Leicester, was an assertive Whig/Liberal Member of Parliament for over 50 years.

He vigorously advocated scientific agriculture, crop rotation and sheep and cattle breeding on his estate. This agricultural revolution helped to feed England's Industrial Revolution. In Ireland, however, the smallholdings and lack of capital delayed scientific farming for a century. Coke did not visit his friend William Palgrave II in Dublin. Indeed, there seems to be no evidence that the Holkham farm influenced early proceedings at the (Royal) Dublin Society after 1750.

As a Whig/Liberal, Coke supported Daniel O'Connell's campaign for Catholic Emancipation in 1829. George IV and his 'Irish' Prime Minister Arthur Wellesley, Duke of Wellington (1769-1852), stubbornly opposed all reform. However, it is unlikely that Coke ever visited Ireland or that the Irish landed gentry inspected the Holkham farm.

In an era of political patronage, it may well be that Coke influenced Palgrave's Dublin appointment *c.*1825. This was the Jane Austen era of social freedoms inhabited by Coke and by George IV with Mrs. Maria Fitzherbert. The severities of Queen Victoria and of Albert were yet to descend on her realm.

THE WHIGS IN IRELAND

The English Whig Party opposed the wars against America and revolutionary France. They advocated moderate political reforms, accountability and curtailment of the power of the Georgian monarchy. Coke of Holkham and the Palgraves, like Edmund Burke, supported Charles James Fox, the Whig leader. In the mid-1830s the 'Whig' Party label was changed to 'Liberal'.

In Ireland the Whig Club was supported by some landed gentry but had a middle-class character. Henry Grattan continued the movement in the United Kingdom parliament after 1800. Daniel O'Connell (1775-1847) co-operated with the Whigs/Liberals to secure a policy of practical reforms within the United Kingdom. His sons reformed The Stephen's Green Club in 1837 to provide a social centre for Liberals on the lines of the Reform Club on Pall Mall in London – see *Whigs on the Green* by Cornelius F. Smith.

What did William Palgrave II make of all this political turmoil when he moved to Dublin about 1826? Was his appointment due to Whig political influence?

—13—

Conclusion

Here ends a social study of two Victorian families and their shipping business. Conclusions are arrived at with sympathy for contemporary outlooks. It has proved difficult to delimit such a history where much primary documentation is no longer available. Some fascinating byways have been explored where they tangentially bear on the main theme, but other interesting contemporary material has been excluded.

> The sea sows savage songs,
> Escape, escape out there
> From familiar September nights,
> Raise anchor for a journey without end,
> Don't stop, move on to turbulence
> From the purlieus of the present,
> There is a future somewhere beyond …
>
> CHRISTOPHER DAY BELL, from *The Fourteen Line Whip*, 1996

The Anna Livia returns to her salty father while gulls call after a lonely steamer.

_14_

Postlude

An elderly captain surveys his ship back home in port. He recalls some wise pilots who charted his course past rocks and sandbanks in 'the mad March days'. The cargo manifest causes him some misgivings. It is of course painful to read in the logbook about the valuable items of cargo and superstructure which are missing – washed overboard by the riptides of time. Like John Masefield's 'dirty British coaster', the goods listed seemed mundane enough when taken on board but what will the market make of it all? This is not a 'quinquireme of Nineveh' or a 'stately Spanish galleon with a cargo of diamonds and gold'. However, there are curiosities and rare artifacts which may delight some cognoscenti.

APPENDIX 14.1

Irish stained glass has been an important element in architecture, linking it with the classic windows of Notre-Dame de Paris, Chartres and other Gothic churches. The Celtic Revival joined in the development of stained glass during the first half of the twentieth century. Typically, the Blackrock windows depict specific saints. The modern cult of abstract geometric shapes and plain colour is not well represented. A new Vatican directory praises authentic art of all styles.

The first church windows were plain glass. Then commercial stained glass was important for the newly built post-Famine churches. In 1903 An Tur Gloine was founded by Miss Sarah Purser (1848-1943) as a co-operative studio. Evie Hone (1894-1955) and many other artists worked there until 1933 when she moved to Marlay Grange. She was commissioned by Senator E. A. McGuire's family in 1954 to produce the three light window in the St. Anne's aisle. It depicts: Madonna & Child, St. Brigid, St. Patrick. This was one of her last works.

The Clarke Studios windows face each other across the centre of the nave. The four-light window on the right facing the sanctuary has the Crucifixion in the top two, and St. Francis of Assisi preaching to the birds in the bottom two.

On the left-hand side, the top two sections depict Our Lady of Mount Carmel presenting the Rosary to St. Simon Stock.

The bottom two are puzzling. The principal figure pierced with arrows is in the style of a St. Sebastian – but clearly is not him. According to Most Rev. N. Donnelly in his *Short Histories of Dublin Parishes*, it commemorates the first curate appointed to the new church, Father Edward Norris. Ordained in 1839, he served for a time on the Indian Mission (American?) where he was scalped! – but survived. He passed to his reward on 12 October 1848.

The Harry Clarke Studios and the Earley Studios were successful in combining artistic skills with mainstream manufacturing facilities. The St. Anne windows in the side aisle were by the Earley Studios in 1932. Harry Clarke (1891-1931), who would have been involved with the designs of the stained glass, has not been credited with its full execution by Dr. Nicola Gordon Bowe in *The Life and Work of Harry Clarke*.

The principal figure in the light window on the left-hand side in the centre of the sanctuary commemorates Father Edward Norris (ordained 1839, died 1848). He served on the American Indian Mission where he was scalped – but survived.
Courtesy Abbey Stained Glass Studios and Michael O'Connell

Other notable stained glass at St. John the Baptist includes the rose window by Wailes of Newcastle over the high altar, presented by Arnold O'Shee in 1843, and the Cloncurry window over the gallery, by Casey (1843). This incorporates the coat of arms of Valentine Browne (1773-1853), 2nd Baron Cloncurry, who had actively supported Daniel O'Connell's campaign for Catholic Emancipation. He lived close by at 'Maretimo', Blackrock.

ACCOUNTS AND FINANCIAL STATEMENTS

		Balances, 31st July, 1886.							
	(Credit Balances)	Forward	1221	16	3	1228	3	9
489	Insurance, City of Hamburg		307	2	3			
491	City of Malaga, Insurance		195	8	7			
493	City of Lisbon "		94	18	9			
495	City of Oporto "		256	9	2			
497	City of Rotterdam "		268	10	1			
499	Minerva "		111	16	9			
528	City of Bristol (1885/86)		166	5	8	2622	7	6
	Credit Balances Ship Ledger.							
216	City of Lisbon 257th Voyage		178	4	3			
322	City of Cadiz 182 "		115	18	2			
359	Minerva 31 "		6	11	10			
360	Minerva 32 "		330	5	4			
433	City of Rotterdam 129 "		78	17	2	704	16	9
503	Sunderland Steam Ship Association					5	7	6
592	Michael Murphy Junr		27	7	2			
591	Thomas Palgrave		14	11	6	41	18	8
	Capital.							
	Charles Palgrave		9041	16	9			
	Michael Murphy		8789	8	9			
	John Murphy		790	0	1			
	James Murphy		828	5	10	19449	11	5
						£24062	5	7

Palgrave Murphy Company Private Ledger abstracts: Profit & Loss Account – voyages – month of June 1886. Balance Sheet as at 31 July 1886.

Memorandum of *Profit and Loss* of **Messrs. Palgrave, Murphy, & Co.'s** *Steamers, 6 Months ending 30th June*

VESSEL.	NATURE OF VOYAGE.	No. of Days.	Disbursements, including Repairs, as per Margin.	Insurance.	Total.	Receipts.	Loss.	Profit.	Repairs.	Folio.	REMARKS
January	From		6642 2 11	867 19 5	7510 2 4	7550 12 9	320 17 4	369 7 9	216 17 8		
February	From		7485 9 9	899 6 5	8384 16 2	9398 9 2	157 1 10	1170 14 10	228 10 10		
March	From		7711 19 4	728 19 5	8440 18 9	8918 7 8	342 1 2	819 10 1	222 12 6		
April	From		6832 2 5	650 16 5	7482 18 10	8441 . 8	199 14 4	1127 16 2	307 7 10		
May	From		8781 12 7	862 15 .	9644 7 7	10188 12 5	462 1 6	1006 1 4	333 14 10		
June	From		6564 9 9	622 9 6	7186 19 3	7945 6 5	210 1 7	968 8 9	139 9 1		
	From		44017 16 9	4632 6 2	48650 2 11	52440 1 1	1692 . 9	5461 18 11	1448 12 9		
May Sheet	From	Minerva Repairs at Glasgow (A & J Inglis)						306 14 1			
June Sheet	From	City of Dortmund Balance of old Cadiz voyage						179 2 2			
do	From	City of Cadiz. Repairs at Dublin (Bewley Webb & Co.)						364 15 4			
	From							252 2 12 4			
	From							£2919 6 7			

The above Profit & Loss Balances have been Correctly Extracted from the Ship Ledgers

Craig Gardner & Co.
27 August 1886

APPENDEX 14.2 B

ULSTER STEAMSHIP COMPANY — REPORT 1909

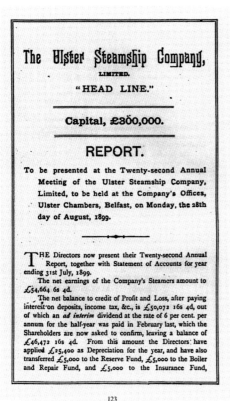

The Ulster Steamship Company,
LIMITED.
"HEAD LINE."

Capital, £300,000.

REPORT.

To be presented at the Twenty-second Annual Meeting of the Ulster Steamship Company, Limited, to be held at the Company's Offices, Ulster Chambers, Belfast, on Monday, the 28th day of August, 1899.

THE Directors now present their Twenty-second Annual Report, together with Statement of Accounts for year ending 31st July, 1899.

The net earnings of the Company's Steamers amount to £54,664 6s 4d.

The net balance to credit of Profit and Loss, after paying interest on deposits, income tax, &c., is £50,072 16s 4d, out of which an *ad interim* dividend at the rate of 6 per cent. per annum for the half-year was paid in February last, which the Shareholders are now asked to confirm, leaving a balance of £46,472 16s 4d. From this amount the Directors have applied £25,400 as Depreciation for the year, and have also transferred £5,000 to the Reserve Fund, £5,000 to the Boiler and Repair Fund, and £5,000 to the Insurance Fund,

123

6

leaving a balance of £6,072 16s 4d, out of which they propose to pay a further dividend at the rate of 6 per cent. per annum for the past six months, making 6 per cent. for the year, free of income tax, and to carry forward the balance, £2,292 16s 4d, to next account.

The Company's Underwriting Account shows a profit for the year of £2,313 12s 7d, which has been added to the Insurance fund.

The Directors having decided to issue the balance of the authorized capital of the Company, offered the remaining 6,000 shares at par *pro rata* to the existing Shareholders, they were largely over-applied for.

The builders, Messrs. Workman, Clark & Co., Limited, expect to give delivery of new twin S.S. "Rathlin Head" during the Autumn.

The Canadian Government have renewed the subsidy granted to the Company for a winter service from Canada to Belfast and Dublin.

All the Steamers of the Company continue to be maintained in the highest state of efficiency. All repairs and renewals have, as heretofore, been defrayed out of revenue.

Mr. Alexander MacLaine, J.P., Chairman, and Mr. A. D. Lemon, J.P. retire from the Directorate by rotation, but are eligible for re-election.

The Auditor, Mr. John Pim, also retires, but offers himself for re-appointment.

By order of the Board,

(Signed)   ALEXANDER MacLAINE,
Chairman.

G. HEYN & SONS, MANAGERS,

ULSTER CHAMBERS,
BELFAST, 15th August, 1899.

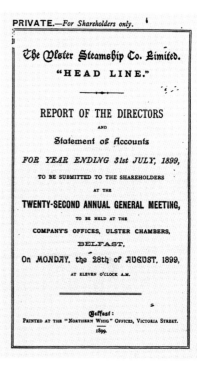

The Ulster Steamship Co. Limited.
"HEAD LINE."

REPORT OF THE DIRECTORS
AND
Statement of Accounts
FOR YEAR ENDING 31st JULY, 1899,
TO BE SUBMITTED TO THE SHAREHOLDERS
AT THE
TWENTY-SECOND ANNUAL GENERAL MEETING,
TO BE HELD AT THE
COMPANY'S OFFICES, ULSTER CHAMBERS,
BELFAST,
On MONDAY, the 28th of AUGUST, 1899,
AT ELEVEN O'CLOCK A.M.

Belfast:
PRINTED AT THE "NORTHERN WHIG" OFFICES, VICTORIA STREET.
1899.

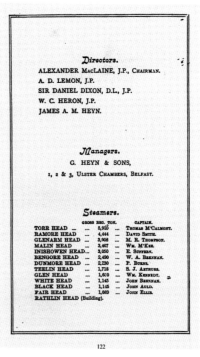

Directors.
ALEXANDER MacLAINE, J.P., CHAIRMAN.
A. D. LEMON, J.P.
SIR DANIEL DIXON, D.L., J.P.
W. C. HERON, J.P.
JAMES A. M. HEYN.

Managers.
G. HEYN & SONS,
1, 2 & 3, ULSTER CHAMBERS, BELFAST.

Steamers.

	GROSS REG. TON.		CAPTAIN.
TORR HEAD	5,910	...	THOMAS M'CALMONT.
RAMORE HEAD	4,444	...	DAVID SMITH.
GLENARM HEAD	3,908	...	M. R. THOMPSON.
MALIN HEAD	3,467	...	WM. M'KEE.
INISHOWEN HEAD	3,050	...	E. SOFFERN.
BENGORE HEAD	2,490	...	W. A. BRENNAN.
DUNMORE HEAD	2,230	...	P. BURNS.
TEELIN HEAD	1,718	...	S. J. ARTHURS.
GLEN HEAD	1,610	...	WM. KENNEDY.
WHITE HEAD	1,145	...	JOHN BRENNAN.
BLACK HEAD	1,145	...	JOHN AULD.
FAIR HEAD	1,089	...	JOHN ELLIS.
RATHLIN HEAD (Building).			

122

The 1909 Report of the Ulster Steamship Company Ltd. is included as an interesting example of the development of marine accounting statements.

Dr.			CAPITAL ACCOUNT.			Cr.
To 24,000 shares, £10—£5 paid		...£120,000 0 0	By Valuation of Company's Steamers at 31st July, 1899	£293,400 0 0		
„ 6,000 shares, £10 (new issue) £1 paid £6,000			*Less* Depreciation now written off	25,400 0 0		
Payments in anticipation of calls 9,876				£268,000 0 0		
	£15,876 0 0		Add Payment to Builders on account new s.s. "Rathlin Head" ...	61,150 0 0		
		£135,876 0 0				£329,150 0 0
„ Reserve Fund, adding ... £5,000	£25,000 0 0		„ Unexpired Insurance...	£12,737 11 0		
„ Boiler & Repair Fund. adding 5,000	23,464 13 5		„ Sundry Debtors, including Insurance Claims under Collection	5,099 11 10		
„ Insurance Fund, adding ... 5,000	26,771 18 10		„ "Head" Line Shed at Montreal, reduced value...	176 13 11		
		75,236 12 3	„ Cash in Bank...	5,246 17 10		
„ Deposits and Temporary Loans ... £125,019 6 2						23,260 14 7
„ Bills payable 10,205 19 10						
		135,225 6 0				
„ Balance		6,072 16 4				
		£352,410 14 7				£352,410 14 7

Dr.			PROFIT AND LOSS ACCOUNT.			Cr.
To Directors' Fees for Year ending 31st July, 1898		£500 0 0	By Balance from last Account ...	£4,611 14 5		
„ Interest Account		5,384 6 5	*Less* Dividend for Half-year ending 31st July, 1898	3,318 18 0		
Ad Interim Dividend paid February, 1899		3,600 0 0				£1,292 16 5
„ Addition to Reserve Fund ... £5,000 0 0			„ Net earnings of Company's Steamers, including Subsidy from Canadian Government and Remuneration for Salvage Services	54,664 6 4		
„ „ „ Boiler and Repair Fund 5,000 0 0						
„ „ „ Insurance Fund 5,000 0 0			„ *Less* Depreciation now written off...	25,400 0 0		
		15,000 0 0				29,264 6 4
„ Balance		6,072 16 4				
		£30,557 2 9				£30,557 2 9

BELFAST, 15th August, 1899.—I have examined the foregoing Balance Sheet and Profit and Loss Account with the Books, Accounts, and Vouchers of the Company and certify same to be correct. As usual the Profit and Loss Account does not include results of a number of voyages completed on or before 31st July, 1899, for which the Managers certify the accounts are not yet made up.

G. HEYN & SONS, *Managers.* J. PIM, *Auditor.*

Dr.			BALANCE SHEET, 31st July, 1909.			Cr.
To Share Capital allotted—30,000 Shares, £10 each— with £6 10s per share paid up		£195,000 0 0	By Valuation of Company's Steamers at 31st July, 1909	£430,000 0 0		
„ Reserve Fund ... £20,000 0 0			*Less* depreciation now written off ...	10,000 0 0		
Less Transferred to depreciation ... 10,000 0 0						£420,000 0 0
	£10,000 0 0		„ Unexpired Insurance	21,423 2 6		
„ Boiler and Repair Fund ... 15,804 8 11			„ Sundry Debtors, including Insurance Claims under collection	10,525 18 7		
„ Insurance Fund 22,107 3 6		47,911 12 5	„ "Head" Line Shed at Montreal ...	180 12 0		
						£32,129 13 1
„ Deposits and Temporary Loans £141,457 11 3						
„ Sundry Creditors 3,251 12 7						
„ Bills Payable 26,387 16 8						
„ Belfast Banking Co., Ltd. ... 32,416 6 2						
„ Outstanding Dividends 20 6 3						
		203,533 12 11				
„ Profit and Loss—Balance at credit per A/c subjoined		5,684 7 9				
		£452,129 13 1				£452,129 13 1

Dr.		PROFIT AND LOSS ACCOUNT, Twelve Months ending 31st July, 1909.			Cr.
To Directors' Fees	£500 0 0	By Balance from last account ...	£6,243 8 11		
„ Interest Account	8,331 6 6	*Less* Dividend for half-year ending 31st July, 1908	4,875 0 0		
„ General Expenses and Income Tax	274 0 8				£1,368 8 11
„ *Ad Interim* Dividend paid February last ...	3,900 0 0	„ Net Earnings of Company's Steamers for completed voyages			17,321 6 0
„ Balance	5,684 7 9				
	£18,689 14 11				£18,689 14 11

A. D. LEMON, } *Directors.*
WM. C. HERON, }

G. HEYN & SONS, *Managers.*

We report to the Shareholders that we have audited the foregoing Balance Sheet of the ULSTER STEAMSHIP Co., LTD., with the books of the Company and the vouchers relating thereto, and have obtained all the information and explanations we have required.

In our opinion the Balance Sheet is a full and fair one, and properly drawn up so as to exhibit a true and correct view of the Company's affairs at the date thereof, according to the best of our information and the explanations given to us, and as shown by the books of the Company. No credit is taken in Profit and Loss Account for a number of voyages which had terminated prior to 31st July, 1909, and for which the accounts are not yet made up.

ARTHUR J. HILL, VELLACOTT, & BAILEY, *Chartered Accountants,*

BELFAST, 19th August, 1909. AUDITORS.

APPENDIX 14.3

BIBLIOGRAPHY — SOURCES ACKNOWLEDGED

★ indicates mentioned in text.

> Seek not to know who said this or that,
> but take note of what has been said,

THOMAS À KEMPIS *Imitation of Christ* VI *c.*1420

★ Alan, Mea	*Palgrave of Arabia*	Macmillan, London	1960
★ Anderson, Ernest B.	*Sailing Ships of Ireland*	Morris & Co., Dublin	1951/
			1984
★ Barry, J.A.	*Queenstown for Orders 1800-1922*	Sidney Publishing, Cork	1999
★ Bowe, Nicola Gordon	*Harry Clarke*	Irish Academic Press	1989
Boylan, Henry	*Dictionary of Irish Biography*	Gill & Macmillan	1998
	History of the Royal Irish Y.C.	A. & A. Farmar	1994
Brady, J. Simms A.	*Dublin Through Space & Time*	Four Courts	2001
Casey, Frank	*Credit were Credit is Due*	Institute of Public Administration	2000
★ Collins, Timothy	*The Galway Line*	Collins Press	2002
Connolly, S.J. (ed.)	*Irish History, Companion*	Oxford U.P.	1998
Cosgrave, E. M.	*Contemporary Dublin Biographies*	Pike	1908
Cowell, John	*Sligo Land of Yeats' Desire*	O'Brien Press	1989
Crookshank, Anne and the Knight of Glin	*Ireland's Painters 1600-1940*	Yale U.P.	2002
★ Cullen, LM.	*Princes and Pirates*	Dublin Chamber of Commerce	1983
★ Daly, Mary	*Dublin, The Deposed Capital 1860-1914*	Cork U.P.	1985
D'Arcy F. and R. Hannigan	*Workers in Union*	National Archives	1988
de Courcey, J.W.	*The Liffey in Dublin*	Gill & Macmillan	1996

★ Duffy, Eamon	*A History of the Popes*	Yale U.P.	1997
Dunleavy, Mairead	*Dress in Ireland – a History*	Collins Press	1999
★ Farmar, A.	*Craig Gardner & Company*	Gill & Macmillan	1988
Farrell, Brian	*The Irish Parliamentary Tradition*	Gill & Macmillan	1973
Findlater, Alex	*Findlaters – 1774-2001*	A. & A. Farmar	2001
Flynn, Arthur	*Ringsend*	Anna Livia Press	1990
Forde, Frank	*Maritime Arklow*	Glendale Press	1988
Foster, R.E., (ed.)	*Illustrated History of Ireland*	Oxford U.P.	1989
Gilligan, Henry A.	*A History of the Port of Dublin*	Gill & Macmillan	1988
★ Harrison, Richard S.	*Irish Insurance 1650-1939*	Privately published	1992
Harvey, W.J.	*The Head Line*	World Ship Society	1990
Healy, Elizabeth (ed.)	*The Book of the Liffey*	Wolfhound Press	1958
Ireland, John de C.	*Ireland in Maritime History*	Glendale Press	1986
Kemp, Peter	*Ships & the Sea*	Oxford U.P.	1976
★ Ketchum, J. Davidson	*Ruhleben, A Prison Camp 1914-18*	Toronto U.P.	1965
★ Lowth, Cormac	*Shipwrecks on the Dublin Coastline*	Blackrock Society	2000
Masefield, John	*Collected Poems*	Heinemann	1923
McCreedy, Rev.C.T.	*Dublin Street Names*	Hodges & Figgis	1892
McGowan, Padraig	*Money Banking in Ireland*	Institute of Public Administration	1990
McNeill, D.B.	*Irish Passenger S.S. Services*	Newtonabbey, Belfast	1969
★ Palgrave, Derek and P. Palgrave-Moore	*History and Lineage of the Palgraves*	Palgrave Society	1978
★ Pearson, Peter	*The Heart of Dublin*	O'Brien Press	2000
	Between the Mountains and the Sea	O'Brien Press	1998
Robbins, Keith	*The Eclipse of a Great Power 1870-1975*	Longman	1983
Robinson, Howard	*A History of Accountants in Ireland*	Institute of Chartered Accountants in Ireland	1983

Rowe, David, (ed.)	*The Irish Chartered Accountants Centenary*	Gill & Macmillan	1988
★ Smellie, John	*Shipbuilding and Repairing in Dublin, 1901-1923*	McCorquodale	1925
Smith, Cornelius F.	*The Royal Irish Automobile Club 1901-91*	R.I.A.C.	1994
	Whigs on the Green	Gill & Macmillan	1990
	Newtownpark Avenue: its people and their houses	Albany Press	2001
★ Smyth, Hazel P.	*B & I Line*	Gill & Macmillan	1984
Somerville-Large, P.	*Dublin*	Granada Publishing	1981
Sterling, A.M.W.	*Coke of Norfolk*	Rare Book – T.C.D.	–
Wigham, M.J.	*The Irish Quakers*	Religious Society of Friends	1992

PERIODICALS AND JOURNALS

Blackrock Society – Record of Proceedings
Books Ireland
Dublin Builder 1857-1966
Dublin Port Year Books
Foxrock Local History Club, publications
Illustrated London News
Ireland of the Welcomes, Bord Failte
Liverpool History Society Journal
Lloyd's Log
Old Dublin Society Record
Sea Breezes
Thom's Directory
Wilson's Directory

APPENDIX 14.4

Grandfather, designated as Michael Murphy I

Son,   designated as Michael Murphy II, J.P.

Grandson,   designated as (Sir) Michael Murphy III

Money –   Changes took place in currency during the period. However, there is no satisfactory equivalent of historical sums of money in today's Irish money.

Pre-decimal £	Slang Names	Decimal £	Euro €
£1 = 240d.	Quid	£1 = 100p	€1 = £0.787564
6d.	Tanner	2.5p	1.2 cent
1s.	Bob	5p	6.3 cent
2s. 6d.	Half-Crown	12.5p	15.9 cent
10s.	Half Note	50p	63.5 cent

TECHNICAL SHIPPING TERMS:

PS   before the name of a ship denotes paddle steamer.

SC   before the name of a ship denotes screw propeller.

SS   before the name of a ship denotes steamship.

MV before the name of a ship denotes motor vessel.

RMS   before the name of a ship denotes Royal Mail Ship.

HMS   before the name of a ship denotes Her Majesty's Ship.

SPC   before the name of a ship denotes Steam Packet Company

PLIMSOLL MARK OR LINE:

A mark painted on the sides of British merchant ships which indicates the draught levels to which a ship may be loaded with cargo for varying conditions of season and location. This mark is accompanied by another, consisting of a circle bisected by a horizontal line with letters which indicate the registration society. In Britain, these are normally LR, indicating Lloyd's Register.

The Plimsoll Mark was made compulsory in Britain under the conditions of the Merchant Shipping Act, 1876, passed after a long and bitter parliamentary struggle conducted by Samuel Plimsoll, M.P., a champion of better conditions for seamen.

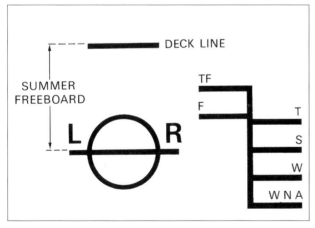

PLIMSOLL MARK AND LOAD LINE

TF   Tropical fresh water

F   Fresh water

T   Tropical sea water

S   Summer, sea water

W   Winter, sea water

WNA Winter.North Atlantic,for vessels under 100 metres (330 feet) in length

LR   These letters indicate the registration society, in this case Lloyd's Register.

NOTE: *The Oxford Companion to Ships & the Sea* by Peter Kemp has proved itself as a guide to technical shipping terms.

ALPHABETICAL LIST OF BRITISH REGISTERED STEAM VESSELS, 1895

Italics denote "Manager" or a "Ship's Husband," appointed under S. 36 of The Merchant Shipping Act, 1876

X denotes a "Managing Owner" appointed under S. 36 of The Merchant Shipping Act 1876

(a) No information received (b) Reported to be sold (c) No further address given

Pa. Paddle Sc. Screw.

PALGRAVE MURPHY SHIPS

Official No.	Name of Ship	International code	Port/Yr Reg.	Where Built	When Built	Iron/ Steel etc.	Length	Brth	Depth	Net Ton	G. Ton	Horse power	Owner/Part-owner X signifies Managing Owner
77386	City of Amsterdam	QSMV	Dublin 1877	Stockton-on-Tees	1877	Iron	220 5	30 2	15 6	52 4	841	120 Sc.	X John Murphy, 17 Eden Quay, Dublin
74555	City of Belfast	QSMV	Dublin 1889	Kirkcaldy	1876	Iron	226 9	29 3	17 5	53 6	895	111 Sc.	X John Murphy, 17 Eden Quay, Dublin.
81439	City of Bristol	WHPS	Dublin 1882	Hartle-Pool	1882	Iron	235 1	32 6	15 7	79 9	1252	150 Sc.	X John Murphy 17 Eden Quay, Dublin
45019	City of Cadiz	VBNG	Dublin 1876	Stockton	1862	Iron	204 4	28 5	17 3	49 1	785	99 Sc.	X John Murphy 17 Eden Quay, Dublin
60574	City of Cork	KDNQ	Dublin 1877	Sunder-land	1871	Iron	229 5	30 0	17 2	65 9	1019	120 Sc.	X John Murphy, 17 Eden Quay, Dublin
54640	City of Dortmund	HRBF	Dublin 1867	South Sockton	1865	Iron	200 5	29 4	17 4	48 9	773	98 Sc.	X John Murphy, 17 Eden Quay, Dublin
81436	City of Hamburg	WFGC	Dublin 1881	Sunder-land	1881	Iron	231 0	32 6	14 5	75 0	1219	150 Sc.	X John Murphy, 17 Eden Quay, Dublin
47988	City of Lisbon	BQWD	Dublin 1876	Deptford	1864	Iron	204 4	26 3	15 9	38 5	636	98 Sc.	X John Murphy, 17 Eden Quay, Dublin
69262	City of Liverpool	MJPK	Dublin 1892	Hull	1873	Iron	246 6	30 0	16 4	74 2	1168	130 Sc.	X John Murphy, 17 Eden Quay, Dublin
62657	City of Malaga	LGVH	Dublin 1873	Sunder-land	1872	Iron	220 0	30 2	16 9	65 0	1026	98 Sc.	X John Murphy, 17 Eden Quay, Dublin
62655	City of Oporto	LFWP	Dublin 1876	Sunder-land	1872	Iron	215 7	30 1	15 4	56 0	874	95 Sc.	X John Murphy, 17 Eden Quay, Dublin
81447	City of Rotterdam	LFWP	Dublin 1883	Govan	1883	Iron	210 0	29 2	12 1	30 3	656	120 Sc.	X John Murphy, 17 Eden Quay, Dublin

MICHAEL MURPHY COMPANY SHIPS

Official No.	Name of Ship	International code	Port/Yr Reg.	Where Built	When Built	Iron/ Steel etc.	Length	Brth	Depth	Net Ton	G. Ton	Horse power	Owner/Part-owner X signifies Managing Owner
99756	Arthur	LFWP	Dublin 1894	Glasgow	1894	Steel	170 4	23 6	14 4	242	511	95 Sc.	X Michael Murphy, 94 North Wall, Dublin
95320	Beatrice	LRBQ	Dublin 1889	Stockton	1889	Steel	208 0	29 1	13 4	304	657	99 Sc.	X Michael Murphy, 94 North Wall, Dublin
58783	Captain Cook	JWCF	Dublin 1873	Willington Quay	1871	Iron	141 0	22 2	10 4	143	247	50 Sc.	X Michael Murphy, Jun, Guild St. Spencer Dock.
89000	Captain McClure	JWCF	Dublin 1885	Glasgow	1885	Iron	169 6	23 6	14 2	304	503	90 Sc.	X Michael Murphy, Jun, Guild St, Spencer Dock
99756	George	JWCF	Dublin 1894	Glasgow	1894	Steel	170 4	23 6	14 4	242	511	95 Sc.	X Michael Murphy, 94 North Wall, Dublin.

N.B. (1) No Sailing Vessels were registered by Palgrave Murphy Group in 1885

Source: Mercantile Navy List 1895

81449	St. Joseph Dublin		Sail	Bath USA	1865		Steel			1138			Xwilliam Murphy, 9 Lower Sackville St.

N.B. (2) 1910 REGISTER

Official No.	Name of Ship	International code	Port/Yr Reg.	Where Built	When Built	Iron/ Steel etc.	Length	Brth	Depth	Net Ton	G. Ton	Horse power	Owner/Part-owner X signifies Managing Owner
76384	City of Brussels	WVBF	Dublin 1899	Middles- brough	1876	Iron	239 8	30 8	16 1	625	1027	118 Sc.	X John Murphy, 17 Eden Quay, Dublin
69365	City of Berlin	MVPT	Dublin 1897	Seacombe	1874	Iron	244 3	30 7	17 4	594	999	150 Sc.	X John Murphy, 17 Eden Quay, Dublin

APPENDIX 14.5B

W.B. and C. PALGRAVE, PALGRAVE and MURPHY and Co.
PALGRAVE MURPHY Ltd. and DUBLIN TENDERS Ltd.

Courtesy J. Spilman "Sea Breezes" 1962.

Name	Gross Tons	Year Built	Remarks
Corcyra, renamed *City of Cadiz 1882*	779	1862	Sold to W. McAllum, London 1919.
Alexandra	581	1863	Sold 1877/78
Anglian, renamed *City of Lisbon.* 1882	633	1864	Sunk in collision with Isle of Man steamer *Douglas,* off New Brighton, Mersey, 1903.
Lord Byron, renamed *City of Dortmund* 1882	758	1865	Sold to J. Johnson, Cardiff, 1922.
Pioneer	1,041	1866	Left fleet 1877/78
Marquis of Lorne, renamed *City of Cork* (I) 1882	1,052	1870	Sold to Ellerman Lines Ltd. 1903.
City of Dublin (I)	1,057	1872	Left fleet 1879.
Borthwick, renamed *City of Malaga,* 1882	1,064	1872	Sold to Greek buyers, 1915.
Marcasite, renamed *City of Oporto* 1882	894	1872	Bought from Culliford & Co. Sunderland, 1876. Sold to Nobels Explosives Ltd, 1914 for use as a hulk
City of Amsterdam (I)	884	1877	Sold to Ellerman Lines Ltd, 1903.
City of Hamburg (I)	1,219	1881	Sold to W. McAllum, London, 1920.
City of Bristol	1,293	1882	Missing on passage from Swansea to Rotterdam, September 1898.
City of Rotterdam	685	1883	Sunk in collision with steamer *Newbiggin* in English Channel on passage Hamburg to Dublin, June 1909.
Europa	676	1862	Acquired by Palgrave Murphy, 1883. Sunk in collision, 1884.
Minerva	676	1862	Built for Pickernell, London, as *Minerva.* Acquired by Palgrave Murphy, 1883. Sold for breaking up to J.J. King & Sons Ltd., Garston 1909.

City of Belfast, renamed	891	1876	Built for John Bacon, Liverpool as *Tutor*. 1883. Sold 1920 to W. McAllum.
City of Liverpool, renamed	1,101	1873	Built for St. Andrew S.S. Co.Ltd. 1893. Sold to Transport and Trading Co. Ltd. (C. Maltrass), London, 1918.
City of Cologne, renamed	994	1881	Acquired by Palgrave, Murphy, 1896 Sold to Transport and Trading Co. (C. Maltrass), London, 1918.
City of Berlin, renamed	999	1874	Acquired by Palgrave, Murphy, 1897 Sunk as blockship at Pernau, 1915. Salved and sold to Estonian Government.
City of Brussels, renamed	1,027	1876	Acquired by Palgrave, Murphy, 1898 Sold to Transport and Trading Co. Ltd. (C. Maltrass), London, 1918.
City of Vienna, renamed	1,080	1885	Built for Cork S.S. Co. Ltd. Cork as *Shieldrake*. Acquired by Palgrave, Murphy, 1899. Sunk in collision in Bristol Channel while on passage from Swansea to Rotterdam, November 1900.
City of Frankfurt, renamed	918	1895	Acquired by Palgrave, Murphy 1900. Wrecked off Brest, March 1922.
City of Stockholm, renamed	1,336	1882	Built for Joseph Hoult, Liverpool as *Benacre*. Sold to John Murphy, Dublin 1900. Transferred to Palgrave Murphy, 1900. Sold to Thordis Shipping Co. Ltd. 1918
City of Munich, renamed	1,384	1879	Acquired by Palgrave, Murphy 1907 Detained at Hamburg during World War I. Sold to Ulster. S.S. Co. Ltd. (G. Heyn and Sons, Ltd) Belfast. Renamed *Wicklow Head*. Returned to Saorstat and Continental in 1934 and renamed *City of Ghent*.
City of Cork (II), renamed	1,301	1880	Sold to Queenstown Dry Docks and Engineering Co. Ltd. as *Maran Head*. Bought by Palgrave Murphy, 1908. Renamed *City of Cork (II)* Sold to Rhydwen S.S. Co. Ltd. Hull, 1918.

APPENDIX 14.5C

Operative from 1st June 1893
The Schedule herein before referred to

Name of Steamer	Number of shares held by Charles George Palgrave
Minerva	24 sixty-fourths
City of Cadiz	28 sixty-fourths
City of Lisbon	28 sixty-fourths
City of Dortmund	26 sixty-fourths
City of Cork	2S sixty-fourths
City of Liverpool	24 sixty-fourths
City of Malaga	2A sixty-fourths
City of Oporto	24 sixty-fourths
City of Belfast	24 sixty-fourths
City of Amsterdam	28 sixty-fourths
City of Hamburg	22 sixty-fourths
City of Bristol	24 sixty-fourths
City of Rotterdam	24 sixty-fourths

Under the Act for the Registering of British Vessels 1825, the property in every ship or vessel of which there is more than one owner was to be divided into sixty-four parts or shares. When a ship was first registered, the new owners took an oath required by this Act declaring the number of shares held. However the subsequent changes in beneficial ownership are less easy to trace.

APPENDIX 14.5D

SHARES OF OWNERSHIP (64THS) IN SOME EARLY STEAMSHIPS.
Palgrave Murphy & Co. Partnership to 1893.

Name of Ship	Date of Register Acquisition	Chas.Palgrave Died 1893	Murphy Family			
			Michael JP II Died 1894	John	James	Michael III Jnr.
City of Cadiz (renamed)	1876	28	28	4	4	Sold 1919
City of Glasgow	1876	32	32	–	–	Missing 1883
City of Lisbon	1873	28	28	4	4	Sank 1903
City of Dublin	1873	32	32	–	–	Wrecked 1878
Lord Byron						
Renamed *Dortmund*	1867	32	32	–	–	Sold 1922
City of Cork	1873	32	32	–	–	Sold 1903
City of Cork	1877	28	28	4	4	
City of Hamburg	1881 Palgrave Murphy & Company					Sold 1920/21
City of Malaga	1882	32	32			Sold 1915
City of Oporto	1882 Palgrave Murphy Company owned 64 shares					Hulk 1915
City of Rotterdam	1877 Michael Murphy Company owned 64 shares					
City of Rotterdam	1883 Palgrave Murphy Company owned 64 shares					Wrecked 1909
Minerva	1883 Palgrave Murphy Company owned 64 shares					Sold – broken up 1909
City of Amsterdam	1877 Michael Murphy Company owned 64 shares					Sold 1906

APPENDIX 14.6

SHIPPING – THE IRISH QUAKERS' CONTRIBUTION
By Maurice J. Wighan

Joseph Robinson Pim
Courtesy Friends Library

In the early 19th century shipping was not far from the people as it is today. Roads were often very uncertain and hazardous, and coastal cargoes carried in small sailing ships were an integral part of trading. Friends had been accustomed to arranging for the shipping of goods for import and export and up the rivers. Many owned ships themselves. Ebenezer Pike in Cork had large shipping interests as had the Lecky family, and Robert Lecky was a builder of iron ships. In Waterford Jacob, Strangman and Watson was the largest of a number of Quaker exporting firms before the 1780s when they lost two ships in St. Eustacia. The British Admiral Rodney took over the port and auctioned off the cargoes of all the ships there claiming that they were trading with the enemy, which perhaps they were: certainly Joseph Jacob never recovered his money or his health after the disaster.

The first boat to be propelled by steam was in 1802 and Friends already interested in shipping were quick to adopt the new technology. In 1822-1825 Joseph Robinson Pim set up the St. George Steam Packet Company in Cork. This company ran the *SS. Lee* to Liverpool and the *Severn* to Bristol, whilst his brother-in-law supplied the insurance for the goods carried. The Quaker companies did not hesitate to compete with each other and the deck passengers of the *Severn* were each given a loaf of bread by way of encouragement!

James Beal was also in Cork shipping and made history by refuting a speech made at a British Association meeting which scorned the possibility of a steam crossing of the Atlantic. Beale said not only could he guarantee a steam-ship already in operation which could make such a crossing but he knew the right man for master. The vessel was J. R. Pim's *Sirius* which left Cork under Capt. Richard Roberts RN on 31st March 1838 and reached New York on 22nd April, the first steam powered vessel to make the journey. In this it was fortunate for it only reached New York a matter of hours before Brunel's Great Western, a much larger ship built for the purpose and taking a much shorter time. James Beale was later a director of the British and American Steam Navigation Co.

The Malcomsons in Waterford, who ran three smart schooners on the Waterford-London route, were also ship builders, building some 47 ships in Waterford at the Neptune Iron Works between 1847 and 1882, both for sail and steam, including the 4,000 ton *William Penn*. They were the first to set up a regular steamship line between London and St.

TOP LEFT:
John R. Wigham Lighthouse
engineer c. 1860.
*Courtesy Belinda Jacob, Friends
Archives.*

TOP:
James Beale of St. George
S.P.Co.; British and American
S.N.G. 1838 and R.J. Lecky &
Co. shipbuilders, Cork.
Courtesy Belinda Jacob

Petersburg. William Malcolmson was chairman of the Lever Line between Galway and the United States and also concerned in the Limerick and Shannon Transport. In Dublin, J. R. Pim was director of the City of Dublin Steam Packet Co. and Dublin Quaker ship builders included Walpole and Webb, later to become Bewley, Webb & Co.

In Ulster John Pim was concerned with the Belfast to Carlisle route and George Pim and Co. were the agents for the Waterford Steamship Co. between Belfast and Liverpool. Another Quaker firm, Richardson Bros., who were sailing ship owners, started the Liverpool Philadelphia Steamship Co. which continued for many years and introduced the plan of cheap steerage fares. These carried passengers across the Atlantic for £5 including accommodation and food. Later the Richardsons, as Friends, refused to charter their ships to the British government during the Crimean war. James N. Richardson and Henry Barcroft were also concerned in the Newry and Dundalk shipping company.

Edmundson's engineering firm, through the interest and invention of the chairman, John R. Wigham★, (1829-1906), made substantial improvements in lighthouse illumination. He was the first to wire a steamship on the Irish Sea route for electricity.

Note: The index indicates further information about most of these shipping Quakers.

APPENDIX 14.7

DUBLIN STREET NAMES – M'CREEDY

The Rev. C.T. M'Creedy, D.D., "Dated and explained the names of the streets" of their Dublin quayside for Charles Palgrave, his partner Michael Murphy, J.P.. II, and their contemporaries.

Note: that M'Creedy lists the bridges and the quays together in order of location on the River Liffey.

Benson-str. (Sir John Rogerson's qu.) 1795

Beresford-pl. 1791. From the Rt. Hon. John Beresford (1738-1805), M.P. for Co. Waterford, Chief Commissioner of the Revenue (1780-1802), The neighbouring Custom Ho. Was built in 1791 by his advice. [See his Correspondence in 2 vols., 1854. Cf. Eden qu].

Blessington-str. (Dorset-str. Up.) 1795. -pi. 1818. -ct. From the Earl of Blessington, cr. 1816, ext. 1829. (He was the eldest s. of the Rt. Hon. Luke Gardiner (1745-98), cr. Baron Mountjoy, 1789, and Viscount Mountjoy, 1795. Cf. The neighbouring Gardiner-str. and Mountjoy-sq).

Blind-quay [not on the river]. 1639. Ir. 1674. -up. 1697. Now known as Exchange.str. and up., q.v. (Cf. Great Britain-quay, a thoroughfare not on any river or canal).

Bloody-br. See under Bridges (Liffey, - Victoria.br.).

BRIDGES

I. Over the Liffey (proceeding from the mouth):-

1. **Butt**-br. (Beresford-pl.) 1879. From Isaac Butt. M.P.. Q.C. [Erected 1879.]

2. **O'Connell**-br. (Sackville-str.) 1880. From Daniel O'Connell, M.P. Formerly called **Carlisle**-br., 1794, from Frederick Howard (1748-1825), 5th Earl of Carlisle, L.L. 1780-82. [Erected, 1794; rebuilt, 1880]

3. **Wellington**-br. (Liffey-str.) 1816. From the Duke of Wellington, who won the battle of Waterloo in 1815. Popularly called the Metal- or the Iron- br., - from the material of which it is made. [Erected in lieu of a ferry, 1816, by Alderman Beresford and Mr. Wm.

(1729) Elizabeth, eldest dau. of Sir John Rogerson, and acquired this property. (Cf. Creighton-str., and Eme-str.)

14. **South-wall**, 1766 [Newspaper ex. In Haliday, cxxii.] From its position at the *south* of the entrance to the river Liffey. It has also been called Ballast-office-wall, - Pigeon-ho.-wall, - Lighthouse-wall, - mall, - mole, or -jettie. (Haliday, 296). The wall from Ringsend to the Pigeon-ho. Fort was completed in 1735. The Poolbeg (q.v.) Light-ho. was completed in 1767, - and the wall connecting it with the Pigeon-ho. was completed in 1790. (Haliday, 237, 238.) The Pigeon-ho.-rd., or -wall, is so called from the Pigeon-ho. there. - which, at first a house for storing wreck, became subsequently a hotel (1790) for persons crossing to or from England, and finally (1798) a fort or magazine, a barrack, and a military port. In 1814, the Government paid the Harbour-board £100,183, for the basin and premises. The name was probably derived from one John *Pigeon*, employed there in 1786. (Haliday, 231. Cf. Dubl. Pen. Jour., ii. 99.) The western end of the Pigeon-house-rd, is called York-rd., - probably so called from York-ter. (1863). [See Blacker's Booterstown, etc., 54.]

II. ON THE GRAND CANAL DOCKS:-

1. **Charlotte**-qu. 1795. From *Charlotte* (1744-1818), queen (m. 1761) of Geo. III.
2. **Grand-Canal**-qu. 1791. From the *Grand-canal*, - opened here in 1791.
3. **Hanover**-qu. 1800. [Map.] From the neighbouring Hanover-str., - of which it is a continuation.
4. **Great Britain**-qu. 1795. From *Great Britain*. See Great Britain-str. This is not what is usually meant by a *quay*, - but it is an ordinary road, connecting Ringsend-br. with Beggar's-bush. It is now called Lots-rd., q.v. [See Blacker's Booterstown, etc., 332.]

   Ringsend-br. See Bridges (Dodder), -rd. The name Ringsend (1673, - de Gomme) is to be derived from the Irish *rinn*, an end or point, - the reference being to the point of land, formerly between the Dodder (1238) and the sea. (Joyce, i. 406.) In Sir Bernard de Gomme's map (Haliday, 229) of 1673, this spit or point is strikingly seen. (The derivation is to be decidedly rejected which would make the name refer to the last of the rings attached to the piles for mooring ships, where Sir John Rogerson's-quay now confines the Liffey. See Blacker's Booterstown, etc., 53.)

Townsend-str.

1. S. (Hawkins-str.) 1674. Perhaps from the *Town's End*? So printed by Andrew Yarranton in 1674. [Haliday, 242]. Formerly called Lazars'-hill, 1657, q.v. 'Lowsey Hill'.

2. N. (Broadstone.) 1776 From George Townshend, 1st Marquis Townshend, – L.L., 1767-72. Formerly called Glasmanoge, 1756, – and now Constitution-hill, 1792.

APPENDIX 14.8

The 1893 Settlement

<u>Special Surveys</u>   When due

City of Amsterdam   No 1   1894

City of Belfast *   No 4   1893

City of Bristol   No 3   1894 (January)

City of Cadiz *   No 1.   1893

City of Cork *   No. 1 (1st) 1893

City of Dortmund   No 1   1893

City of Hamburg (partially thing No 3   1893

City of Lisbon *   No 1   1893

City of Liverpool *   No 1   Jany 1895

City of Malaga   No 1   1896

City of Oporto   No 2   1893

City of Rotterdam   No 3   1895

Minerva   *   No 2   1896

t...g and Annual
...ing how due on
...ves marked *
...he text month *

Valuation of the thirteen ships on dissolution of partnership occasioned by the death of Charles George Palgrave on 26 May 1893.
See Chapter 7.1 (A).

Courtesy National Archives of Ireland

Analysis of Valuation made

by John Preston & Co Cornhill, London

boiler	Name	age	deadweight	Value per ton			Value gross	
16	Minerva	31	800	3	7	6	2700	~ ~
17	C. Cadiz	31	900	3	6	8	3000	~ ~
19	C. Lisbon	29	750	3	6	8	2500	~ ~
18	C. Dortmund	28	950	3	3	2	3000	~ ~
16	C. Cork	23	1250	3	4	~	4000	~ ~
11	C. Liverpool	21	1370	3	8	2	4670	~ ~
11	C. Malaga	21	1300	2	17	8	3750	~ ~
11	C. Oporto	21	1000	3	15	~	3750	~ ~
11	C. Belfast	17	1240	4	0	7	5000	~ ~
12	C. Hamburg	12	1350	4	16	3	6500	~ ~
11	C. Bristol	11	1450	4	15	2	6900	~ ~
10	C. Rdam	10	800	6	17	6	5500	~ ~
16	C. Amsterdam	16	1000	4	2	~	4100	~ ~
			14.660				£55.370	~ ~

Average price per ton £ 3 18 2
Average age of steamers 20 11/13 years
Average age of tonnage 20 years
Average age of boilers 13 8/13 years

Gross Register Tonnage of above steamers
117.41 tons Valuation per ton gross £ 4143

14.9 INDEX

I propose to bring a bill into Parliament to deprive an author who publishes a book without an index of the privilege of copyright, and, moreover to subject him for his offence to a pecuniary penalty.

LORD JOHN CAMPBELL (1779-1861)
Lives of Chief Justices, III, Preface

(Names of ships and steamers, Songs and books are italicised)